INSTANTLY
Southern

INSTANTLY
Southern

85 Southern Favorites for Your
Pressure Cooker, Multicooker, and Instant Pot®

SHERI CASTLE

Photography by Hélène Dujardin

CLARKSON POTTER / PUBLISHERS
NEW YORK

Published in the United States by Clarkson Potter/Publishers,
an imprint of the Crown Publishing Group, a division
of Penguin Random House LLC, New York.
clarksonpotter.com | crownpublishing.com

CLARKSON POTTER is a trademark and POTTER with colophon
is a registered trademark of Penguin Random House LLC.

Library of Congress Cataloging-in-Publication Data
Names: Castle, Sheri, author.
Title: Instantly Southern : 85 Southern favorites for
your pressure cooker, multicooker, and Instant Pot / Sheri Castle.
Description: First edition. | New York : Clarkson Potter/Publishers, [2018] | Includes index.
Identifiers: LCCN 2018020622| ISBN 9781984822475 (trade pbk.) | ISBN 9781984822482 (ebook)
Subjects: LCSH: Cooking, American--Southern style. | Pressure cooking. | LCGFT: Cookbooks.
Classification: LCC TX715.2.S68 C3848 2018 | DDC 641.5975-dc23 LC
record available at https://lccn.loc.gov/2018020622

ISBN 978-1-9848-2247-5 • Ebook ISBN 978-1-9848-2248-2

Printed in U.S.A.

Book and cover design by Casalino Design Inc
Book and cover photographs by Hélène Dujardin

10 9 8 7 6 5 4 3 2 1

First Edition

For Lily, my favorite person in this world.

Ain't that just the way?

Contents

Introduction

I believe in multicookers because I believe in home cooking. It's why I wrote this book.

I wasn't an early adopter of multicookers. For months I listened to friends and colleagues rave about their pots, eager to tell me all about how easy they are to use and how recipes were turning out quicker and better than ever. I read the magazine articles and viral social media posts. And yet I didn't buy one right away—I wasn't sure I needed one. I didn't understand that a multicooker isn't just another appliance; it's a whole new way to cook.

Curiosity got the better of me, and I bought one. By the end of the first week, I was a devoted convert. I embraced (and rejoiced!) that I can use my pot to make fabulous Southern recipes and have them turn out as good as, if not better than, the way I'd always done them, not to mention faster and often easier.

I wrote *Instantly Southern* to share my enthusiasm with fellow cooks (at all skill levels) who are cooking in a variety of circumstances. A multicooker is a smart addition to a large, well-stocked kitchen, as well as a brilliant solution for cooks with modest kitchens, or no kitchen at all, perhaps while traveling or living in a studio apartment, dorm room, or temporary housing. With nothing more than simple groceries and access to an outlet, people can use a multicooker to prepare complete meals, and delicious ones at that. That's a godsend.

Now let's talk about some Southern recipes for your multicooker. When deciding what to include in *Instantly Southern*, I aimed for a mix of classic and brand new recipes that reveal the range of dishes and ingredients that work well in a multicooker. I made classic dishes such as Chicken and Sausage Jambalaya (page 19), Texas Bowl of Red (page 79), and Chicken and Fluffy Dumplings (page 85 and in the photo opposite). I gave fresh twists to familiar favorites, such as Salted Caramel Banana Pudding (page 158), and Granola Porridge (page 49). I used the speed of pressure-cooking to make things more quickly and easily, such as Quick Greens (page 132), and 5-Minute Mac and Cheese (page 95). I embraced the slow-cooking option for dishes such as Pulled Chicken Sandwiches in Cheerwine Barbecue Sauce (page 101) and Meaty Cowboy Beans (page 37). I marveled at the automation that let me make things with the press of a button, such as Fresh Cottage Cheese (page 125) and Buttermilk Ricotta (page 47). There are meals for all occasions, from school-night casual (Cheeseburger Casserole, page 87) to a dinner party (Bourbon and Cola Beef Short Ribs, page 105) to dessert (Pineapple Upside-Down Cake, page 153). Most of the recipes can be made entirely in the pot, but some require an oven (to melt a cheesy casserole topping or bake a pie shell) or another small appliance (such as a blender, to finish a sauce).

Instantly Southern reflects my many eye-opening successes. I had fabulous aha moments that made me snap photos to send to my friends and post online. Every success made me more eager and confident about experimenting with new things and love my pot even more. I'll admit that some things I tried didn't work. The pots work wonders, but they cannot crank out crisp or crusty browned food. There will be no fried chicken, skillet cornbread, or hot biscuits from a multicooker, at least not yet.

I encourage everyone who uses *Instantly Southern* to follow the instructions—not to be tedious, but rather to be successful. I included plenty of tips, hints, and insights to help others avoid the mistakes and pitfalls that I faced when I was learning to make the best use of my pot and adapt my favorite recipes. Each of us continues to learn more about our pots each time we use them and try something new, and it's fun to share information and recipes with my fellow multicooker enthusiasts.

Southern food is broad, diverse, intensely local, and evolving. There are many delicious, authentic, creative ways to stir a Southern pot, including electric ones. Despite that, some people think that if a dish or recipe didn't originate on their granny's table, then it can't possibly be Southern, and they dismiss it. That's a shame. If my version of a classic is different from yours, rather than be critical, why not try it? Make the recipe as I've written it, and then adapt it to reflect your preferences and family recipes. Before you know it, you'll know exactly how to prepare many of your heirloom recipes, and create new ones to pass along.

Yes, a multicooker is new to many of us, but there's nothing new about curious Southern cooks' eagerness and willingness to embrace new techniques, conveniences, and ingredients—even new ways of

thinking. Storied food, world-class cooking, and sharing meals in fellowship with friends and family are among the most enjoyable and treasured Southern traditions. A multicooker will help, so let it.

Good Advice for Using Your Multicooker

Pots from different manufacturers (and pots from the same manufacturer that evolve through upgrades) might work a bit differently and use different terminology. There can be a learning curve at first, but it will soon feel familiar and easy, like learning to drive. If you misplace the manual, fear not. Go to the manufacturer's website, do an online search of the make and model to pull up a copy, or call the manufacturer's hotline (most have one).

Terms Used in This Book

Different manufacturers and models might have slightly different terminology and functions from the words I use in my recipes. As with any new appliance, **I highly recommend reading your user manual** so that you know how to use your multicooker safely and effectively.

PRESSURE COOKING

High Pressure and **Low Pressure** are manual settings on the pot. The recipe will instruct you on the proper pressure level and cooking time. Some function buttons (such as **Soup/Broth** or **Meat/Stew**) are other ways to select pressure-cooking. Function buttons offer suggested default cooking times that you can accept or adjust manually. It's my experience that default times are not as precise as those in recipes. The pot cannot magically intuit your recipe and assess doneness, so it's preferable to trust your recipe and manually select the pressure level and cooking time.

The cooking time in pressure-cooking recipes is only the time the food will cook under pressure. The length of time for the entire cycle (from when you lock the lid to when it unlocks so that you can remove it) varies widely depending on things such as the contents of the pot, the strength of the pressure, and how long the food cooked under pressure. You cannot control or adjust how quickly the pressure builds or naturally releases, although you can monitor it on a digital display on some multicookers.

The valve on top of the pot must be closed in order for the pot to build up pressure. Some pots require the valve to be closed manually. On others, the valve closes automatically when the lid locks in place.

Some pots use a small metal pin to indicate when pressure-cooking has started and ended. The pin rises at the start of the cooking cycle and drops when all of the pressure is released from the pot and you can unlock and remove the lid. Other pots also have a digital display on the front that allows you to monitor each stage of cooking.

Pressure-cooking requires liquid. Follow the instructions in the recipe and measure carefully.

COVER

The multicooker lid must be locked in place for pressure-cooking. Most pots give an error message when the lid is ajar. After cooking, as a safety feature, the pot's lid will remain locked and cannot be removed until all the pressure is released. When using nonpressure-cooking functions, you can use a tight-fitting tempered glass lid (see page 14). Some functions, such as **Sauté** and **Warm**, can be used in an open, uncovered pot.

RELEASE

The steam that builds up during pressure-cooking must be released at the end of cooking before you can remove the lid. There are two types: **Natural Release** and **Quick Release**. Always follow the times specified in a recipe for **Natural Release** or **Quick Release** because they affect whether the food will turn out properly cooked. The food inside the pot continues to cook until all steam is released and the lid can be removed.

• Natural Release begins automatically at the end of pressure-cooking. The length of time it takes for all of the pressure to be released naturally varies, depending on things such as how long the pot has been under pressure and the contents of the pot. You cannot adjust or control the speed of **Natural Release**, although on some multicookers you can monitor all cooking cycles on a digital display. You can let the pot stand for a full **Natural Release** or you can interrupt the **Natural Release** at any time and then use a **Quick Release** of any remaining pressure. Follow the instructions and times in your recipe. Many recipes begin with a **Natural Release** followed by a **Quick Release.**

• Quick Release is when you choose to release all of the pressure inside the pot at once. Some recipes call for **Quick Release** immediately after the end of pressure-cooking to release the steam as quickly as possible. Other recipes call for a **Quick Release** of any remaining pressure after the specified length of **Natural Release**. To initiate **Quick Release**, you must manually open the valve on top of the pot. Refer to your user manual to understand your model and understand how to release pressure safely and accurately. Always protect yourself from the hot steam when opening a valve.

STEAM AND SAFETY

The amount of steam the pot emits during a pressure release varies, depending on whether the food was cooked on **High** or **Low Pressure**, the length of cooking time, the contents, and the fullness of the pot. It might take several minutes for a large recipe cooked for more than an hour on **High Pressure** to **Quick Release** all of its steam, and that steam will blow out vigorously at first. In contrast, a recipe cooked on **Low Pressure** for only a minute will release little steam. Any length of **Natural Release** reduces the amount of pressure left for **Quick Release**. Total **Natural Release** emits no steam blast. To diffuse and absorb some of the steam blast so that it doesn't spray all over the cabinets and counters, loosely drape a towel over the open valve, making sure it doesn't block or impede the valve.

BURN WARNING MESSAGE

One of the safety features of multicooker pressure-cooking is that some models issue a **Burn** message if the food inside the pot begins to scorch. Should that occur, **Quick Release** the pressure so that the lid will unlock and you can remove it. Then stir vigorously to loosen the food from the bottom of the pot, adding a splash of water if necessary if the mixture is too thick, and then resume the cooking cycle. Sometimes, unfortunately, so much food has stuck and burned that it can't be salvaged. I noted recipes in this book that are vulnerable to sticking, along with a reminder to stir well. Always precisely measure liquids (and all ingredients) when using a multicooker, including any water poured into the pot.

Cleaning Your Pot

Not all brands of multicooker have removable stainless steel inner pots, but if yours does, it is usually the only component that is dishwasher safe and immersible. Be sure the outside is dry before returning it to the cooker. Use a damp towel to wipe down the rest of the cooker.

Be sure that the rim of the inner pot and the inside of the lid are dry and free of debris, which can interfere with the lid sealing. Those spots can get grimy and sticky, especially after sautéing fatty foods or cooking starchy dishes. It's a tight squeeze, so you might want to use a toothbrush reserved for this purpose or a damp paper towel wrapped around the end of a chopstick to get in there.

Inspect the sealing ring each time you use the multicooker to ensure that it is securely hooked into place. Rings must be removed and washed regularly, lest they harbor odors and aromas from the previous recipe. I store my lid inverted on the pot when not in use so that the ring can air out and dry completely between uses.

Useful Must-Haves and Handy Add-Ons

Purchasing a few accessories for your multicooker is a smart investment. They make some tasks easier and safer for a nominal additional cost. Before using an accessory you already have on hand or when purchasing new accessories, be sure that they will fit and function inside your pot.

OVEN MITTS

Multicookers get hot, as does the food inside them, and the steam that shoots out when the pressure is released. Sturdy oven mitts are nearly as important as common sense and good judgment when it comes to multicookers. I rely on glove-style mitts that let me use my fingers as part of my grip.

STEAMER BASKET

A steamer basket is necessary for some recipes. The least expensive option is a collapsible basket that unfolds like a flower, but because it has no sides, the capacity is limited and food can easily tumble into the pot. I prefer a deep wire-mesh basket with a sturdy handle.

METAL TRIVET WITH HANDLES

All pots come with metal trivets that can hold food and pot-in-pot dishes above the water in the bottom of the pot. Some trivets do not have handles to hold when lowering and lifting food and dishes in and out of the pot—in that case, you can use a sling made from folded aluminum foil, but I recommend buying a trivet with handles, as they are safer and easier to use than a foil sling. Plus, many trivets can be folded flat when not needed, making them easy to tuck away and store.

EGG RACK

Egg racks hold eggs in place so that they don't collide during cooking. They often come in two pieces so that you can prepare a dozen or more eggs at once.

TEMPERED GLASS LID

This is different from the multicooker's heavy lid that must be locked in place for pressure-cooking. For functions that do not require a locked lid, such as **Yogurt** and **Sauté**, a lightweight, tempered glass lid is very useful. It's important that the glass lid fits snugly and securely, so purchase a lid that is sized appropriately for your pot.

EXTRA INNER POT

If you use your multicooker to prepare more than one dish during meal preparation (for example, Shrimp and Stoneground Grits, page 26) and don't want to wash the pot between recipes, it's handy to have an extra inner pot at the ready. (Note that not all brands of multicooker have removable inner pots; for this reason, when shopping for a multicooker, I highly recommend you buy one with a removable inner pot.)

POT-IN-POT DISHES

Pot-in-pot (PIP) cooking is the term for putting a second dish, such as a baking dish or baking pan, inside the pot where it sits on a trivet that holds it above the water required for pressure-cooking. The size and shape of the dish or pan is critical. Round dishes and pans that are about 7 inches in diameter fit inside 6-quart pots with enough space on the sides to accommodate the handles of the metal trivet. The dishes and pans can be ceramic, metal, tempered glass, or silicone, but do not use any dish, pan, or glassware that is not ovensafe. Although many cooks have to purchase 7-inch pans (an uncommon size for baking) to use in their pots, many of us have 1½-quart baking dishes, such as Pyrex or CorningWare, that work well. Many manufacturers sell accessories that are guaranteed to work safely and accurately in their pots. Most of the pieces are round, although some are experimenting with loaf and mini muffin shapes.

All PIP pressure-cooking requires water in the pot. Always cover PIP dishes as instructed in the recipe (usually with aluminum foil) so that dripping condensation will not dilute, waterlog, or potentially ruin the food. Also be aware that there can be quite a bit of water clinging to the underside of the pot lid when it is removed after pressure-cooking, so use caution when removing it so that the water doesn't spill or drip all over your countertop and floor.

TONGS

These are the perfect tool for moving large pieces of food in and out of the pot and for turning them as they cook.

JAR LIFTERS

Think of these as oversize tongs that can securely grip jars and ramekins as you move them in and out of the pot.

SPIDER

This is a mesh strainer with a long handle that you can use to scoop out and strain hot, cooked food. For example, you can remove cooked meat and vegetables and leave behind the cooking liquid without having to pour the hot food through a sieve or colander. They work like a slotted spoon, but have a wider, deeper capacity.

A Little Recipe Advice

I used several different models of popular brands of 6-quart multi-cookers to develop these recipes. They all work more or less the same way, but always consult the user manual to learn the particulars of your pot.

As with all appliances, multicookers have quirks. (For example, one of mine consistently runs a little hot, making it more prone to issue the burn warning message, page 13.) You'll learn more about the idiosyncrasies of your pot each time you use it, and can then use those insights to make any necessary minor adjustments the next time you make that recipe.

Cooking times in this book do not include the amount of time that it takes the multicooker to come up to pressure or for a full natural release. That's because there are too many variables, such as the type and density of the food, the ratio of liquids to solids, and the starting temperature of the food, the amount of liquid, altitude, and on and on. Some cookers have a digital display on the front that will let you monitor the rise and fall of the pressure, but you cannot control the speed at which it does this.

Recipes give reliable advice and instructions, but there are always going to be variations in how things might turn out for you. Little things matter: the age and size of dried beans, for example, or even different brands of com-mon grocery items. If you ever have doubt about a cooking time, start with less time. You can always cook a recipe longer, but there is no turning back from overcooked food. If a recipe turns out only a bit undercooked or not as thick as you like, the best option is usually to simmer it uncovered on the SAUTÉ func-tion. If the food is significantly undercooked, it might need more pressure-cooking.

I often include the instruction to "adjust the seasoning" before serving a dish. I use that phrase to cover not only salt, but also pepper, hot sauce, citrus juice, vinegar, sugar, or any ingredient in the recipe that might need a little final refinement to ensure a balanced dish that tastes just right to you. Trust your palate.

Beans, Grains & Grits

Chicken and Sausage Jambalaya

Jambalaya is a one-pot feast made with rice, meat, and vegetables that simmer together until the rice plumps and the flavors mingle, which takes mere minutes in a multicooker, like magic. There are two main categories of jambalaya: Creole and Cajun. Creole is red from tomato while Cajun is staunchly tomato-free. By that measure, this is a Cajun jambalaya.

2 tablespoons vegetable oil

12 ounces andouille sausage, cut into ½-inch-thick rounds

2 medium yellow onions, diced (about 3 cups)

1 medium red bell pepper, cut into 1-inch pieces (about 1½ cups)

1 medium green bell pepper, cut into 1-inch pieces (about 1½ cups)

2 celery stalks, chopped (about ½ cup)

3 large garlic cloves, finely chopped

2 teaspoons Cajun or Creole seasoning

1 teaspoon dried oregano

1 teaspoon ground black pepper

1 dried bay leaf

1¼ cups long-grain white rice

2 pounds boneless, skinless chicken thighs, cut into 2-inch chunks

2½ cups chicken stock, home-made (page 64) or store-bought

2 tablespoons Worcestershire sauce

½ cup chopped fresh flat-leaf parsley

1. Warm the oil in the pot on **SAUTÉ MEDIUM**. Add the andouille and cook until browned, about 5 minutes, stirring often. Use a slotted spoon to transfer the sausage to a bowl.

2. Stir in the onions, red pepper, green pepper, and celery. Cook until the mixture softens, about 3 minutes. Stir in the garlic, Cajun seasoning, oregano, black pepper, and bay leaf. Cook until fragrant, about 1 minute, stirring constantly.

3. Stir in the rice and cook until it is coated in the vegetable mixture, about 1 minute, stirring constantly. Stir in the chicken, stock, and Worcestershire.

4. Cover and cook on **HIGH PRESSURE** for 10 minutes. Let stand for **NATURAL RELEASE** for 10 minutes, then **QUICK RELEASE** the remaining pressure.

5. Stir in the reserved sausage and parsley and let stand uncovered for 5 minutes. Taste and adjust the seasoning, if desired.

> HINT *Creole seasoning is a seasoned salt that includes dried chiles, herbs, and cayenne. Cajun seasoning sometimes contains more cayenne but is so similar that the two can be used interchangeably in most recipes.*

Herbed Farro Salad

Farro has been grown for generations in small pockets of the South where it was used as a rotation crop for rice. The whole grain has a nutty, earthy flavor and pleasantly chewy texture. Warm farro absorbs the flavors in the dressing as it cools, which sets the stage for the crisp, colorful vegetables and herbs.

VINAIGRETTE

¼ cup sherry vinegar

1 tablespoon Dijon mustard, preferably whole-grain

3 garlic cloves, finely chopped

2 teaspoons dried Italian seasoning

2 teaspoons honey or sugar

¼ teaspoon red pepper flakes

½ cup extra-virgin olive oil

Kosher salt and ground black pepper

SALAD

1 cup farro, rinsed (not parboiled or instant)

Kosher salt

2 cups cherry or grape tomatoes, halved

1 cup fresh or thawed petite green peas or shelled edamame (about 4 ounces)

1 cup thinly sliced cucumber half-moons

½ cup pitted Kalamata olives, halved

½ cup thinly sliced roasted red peppers

2 ounces feta cheese, crumbled (about ½ cup)

Ground black pepper

1 cup loosely packed baby arugula

½ cup fresh basil leaves, thinly sliced

> ### HINT
> *This is a great make-ahead salad to enjoy throughout the week or to brown-bag for a lunch. If you plan on setting some aside for another day, wait to add the arugula and basil until shortly before serving so the vinaigrette won't blacken and wilt the tender leaves.*

1. **For the vinaigrette:** Whisk together the vinegar, mustard, garlic, Italian seasoning, honey, and pepper flakes in a medium bowl. Whisk in the oil. Season with salt and black pepper to taste.

2. **For the salad:** Add the farro to the pot with 3 cups water and 1 teaspoon salt. Cover and cook on **HIGH PRESSURE** for 10 minutes. Let stand for **NATURAL RELEASE** for 5 minutes, then **QUICK RELEASE** the remaining pressure.

3. Drain the farro and pour it into a large bowl. Stir in ½ cup of the vinaigrette and let stand until cooled to room temperature, stirring occasionally.

4. Stir in the tomatoes, peas, cucumber, olives, roasted peppers, and feta. Stir in enough of the remaining vinaigrette to moisten the salad; you might have a little left over. Season with salt and pepper, then stir in the arugula and basil.

Barley, Peach, and Cherry Salad
with Sweet Tea Vinaigrette

MAKES 6 SERVINGS

Fresh peaches ripe enough to perfume the kitchen are best for this recipe, but when the craving strikes outside of prime peach season, frozen slices work well. Mild, tender barley is easy to cook and love in this refreshing summer salad dressed in a Southern sweet tea vinaigrette made by steeping black tea in vinegar.

SWEET TEA VINAIGRETTE

½ cup unseasoned rice vinegar or white wine vinegar

3 tablespoons sugar

3 regular-size black tea bags

1 small shallot, finely chopped

Finely grated zest and juice of 1 lemon

¼ cup extra-virgin olive oil

Kosher salt and ground black pepper

SALAD

1 cup pearled barley (not parboiled or instant)

Kosher salt

2 medium peaches, peeled, pitted, and thinly sliced

1 cup cherries, pitted and halved

Ground black pepper

½ cup pecan pieces, toasted if you like

¼ cup coarsely chopped fresh mint leaves

1. **For the sweet tea vinaigrette:** Warm the vinegar and sugar in a very small saucepan over low heat, stirring to dissolve the sugar (or warm the vinegar and sugar in a microwave-safe glass bowl). Remove from the heat and add the tea bags, pressing them into the vinegar mixture to make sure they are saturated. Cover and set aside for 15 minutes. Remove the bags, squeeze gently to get out all of the liquid, and then discard. Whisk in the shallot, lemon zest, lemon juice, and oil, and then season to taste with salt and pepper.

2. **For the salad:** Stir together the barley, 3 cups water, and ½ teaspoon salt in the pot. Cover and cook on **HIGH PRESSURE** for 10 minutes. **QUICK RELEASE** the pressure.

3. Drain the barley and transfer to a large bowl. Stir in the vinaigrette. Let stand until cooled to room temperature, about 20 minutes, stirring occasionally.

4. Stir in the peaches and cherries. Let stand for 5 minutes to give the fruit time to absorb some of the vinaigrette, stirring occasionally. Season to taste with salt and pepper.

5. Just before serving, stir in the pecans and mint. Serve at room temperature. This salad is also nice lightly chilled before serving.

Appalachian Soup Beans

Soup beans are not pretty, but they are beautiful to those of us who hail from the Appalachian Mountains and eat them religiously. Because the cooking liquid is not drained from soup beans (it thickens into a rich, thick sauce), the pintos cook in less water than used in most dried bean recipes. Most devotees prefer soup beans made at least one day ahead and reheated, served with the best skillet cornbread you can make, and often garnished with a smattering of raw onion or chow-chow, which is a colorful, tangy, pickled vegetable relish.

1 pound dried pinto beans, rinsed

1 medium yellow onion, finely chopped (about 1½ cups)

¼ cup bacon fat (see Hint below)

Kosher salt and ground black pepper

HINT
If you need to cook bacon to get the fat for this recipe, you'll need about 4 ounces of bacon, or about 4 thick-cut slices. The cooked bacon isn't usually stirred into the soup beans before serving, although you can.

1. Stir together the beans, 5 cups water, onion, bacon fat, 2 teaspoons salt, and 1 teaspoon pepper in the pot. Cover and cook on **HIGH PRESSURE** for 40 minutes. Let stand for **NATURAL RELEASE** of the pressure.

2. Uncover and simmer the beans on **SAUTÉ MEDIUM** until they are very soft and the cooking liquid has reduced into a thick, opaque sauce that barely covers the beans, 15 to 20 minutes, stirring occasionally. Reduce the heat to **SAUTÉ LOW** if the beans begin to boil. Stir more often as the sauce thickens.

3. Taste for salt and adjust, if desired. Season the beans generously with pepper. Be bold. It is nearly impossible to add too much black pepper to Appalachian food. Turn off the heat and let stand for at least 15 minutes before serving warm. The beans will continue to thicken as they rest.

DELICIOUS, JUDICIOUS BACON FAT

Many Southern cooks keep a container of bacon fat on hand, rendered from bacon that is so smoky that you can smell its aroma even before it is cooked. When you need to cook bacon to get the fat for a recipe, you'll get about 1 tablespoon of rendered fat from 1 ounce of bacon. The size of the packaged bacon slices varies, but most thick-cut slices weigh about 1 ounce.

Chicken Bog

Chicken bog is a type of Southern chicken and rice, but that meager description skips over its nuances and charms. Bog is a celebration of simple chicken and rice—and don't go mistaking simple for bland or insufficient. This comforting dish is like the best type of grandma food that makes us feel better, no matter how good we already feel. Because this recipe takes advantage of a rotisserie chicken, this dish is ready to serve in about a half hour. The chicken does double duty here, providing tender meat for the bog and roasted bones and skin to enrich store-bought chicken broth in only 20 minutes. Be sure to use a chicken that is seasoned with only salt and pepper instead of a bold seasoning that would add unwanted flavors to the dish.

1 plain rotisserie chicken (seasoned with salt and pepper only)

6 cups store-bought chicken broth or stock

1 tablespoon distilled white or apple cider vinegar

1 cup long-grain white rice

2 tablespoons unsalted butter

Kosher salt

1 teaspoon ground black pepper

Juice of 1 lemon (about 3 tablespoons)

1 bunch scallions (white and tender green parts only), thinly sliced (about ¼ cup)

3 tablespoons finely chopped fresh flat-leaf parsley

1. Pull the meat from the chicken and shred it into large bite-size pieces, reserving the skin and carcass for the stock. Cover and refrigerate the meat until needed.

2. Place the skin and carcass in the pot. Add the broth and vinegar. Cover and cook on **HIGH PRESSURE** for 20 minutes. Let stand for **NATURAL RELEASE** of the pressure.

3. Strain the stock through a fine-mesh sieve into a large bowl. Discard the solids. Rinse and dry the pot, return it to the multi-cooker, and add the stock back to it.

4. Stir in the reserved chicken, the rice, butter, 1 teaspoon salt, and the pepper. Cover and cook on **HIGH PRESSURE** for 4 minutes. Let stand for **NATURAL RELEASE** for 10 minutes, then **QUICK RELEASE** the remaining pressure.

5. Stir in the lemon juice. Taste and adjust the seasoning, if desired. Serve warm, topped with scallions and parsley.

Shrimp and Stoneground Grits

The dish known as shrimp and grits is familiar in the South, seen regularly on menus ranging from diners to fine dining. High-quality stoneground grits prepared with care have the unmistakable flavor and aroma of toasted corn, and a multicooker gives them slow-simmered flavor in mere minutes without constant stirring and pot watching. Be sure to buy shell-on shrimp, as the shells are used to make a quick shrimp stock needed for the delicate sauce. And don't forget to do right by the grits. A little cream cheese, although untraditional, keeps the hot grits smooth and creamy.

GRITS

2 cups whole milk

2 tablespoons unsalted butter, plus more to taste

Kosher salt

1½ cups coarse stoneground grits

¼ cup cream cheese, at room temperature (2 ounces)

Ground black pepper

HINT *Coarse grits worked best in a multicooker because fine, powdery grits are prone to sinking and sticking, which can the cause the multicooker to issue the burn warning message. If that happens,* QUICK RELEASE *the pressure so that you can remove the lid, and stir well to loosen to the grits from the bottom of the pot. Instead of resuming pressure-cooking, simmer the grits uncovered on* SAUTÉ LOW *until tender and creamy, stirring often.*

1. **For the grits:** Stir together the milk, 2 cups water, 2 tablespoons butter, and 1½ teaspoons salt in the pot. Bring to a simmer on **SAUTÉ MEDIUM**. Whisking constantly, add the grits in a slow, steady stream. Cover and cook on **HIGH PRESSURE** for 9 minutes. Let stand for **NATURAL RELEASE** for 5 minutes, then **QUICK RELEASE** the remaining pressure.

2. Stir the grits until smooth, taking care to scrape the bottom and sides of the pot where the grits will be the most thick and dense. Add the cream cheese and pepper to taste. Taste and adjust the seasoning, if desired. The grits cannot be bland, so don't skimp on salt, pepper, and butter. Set aside, covered, to keep warm.

3. **For the shrimp:** Warm the oil in the pot on **SAUTÉ MEDIUM**. Stir in the shells and cook until bright pink, about 1 minute, stirring constantly. Add the stock and lemon zest. Cover and cook on **HIGH PRESSURE** for 1 minute. Let stand for **NATURAL RELEASE** of the pressure. Strain the stock into a large bowl and set it aside. Discard the solids. Rinse and dry the pot and return it to the multicooker.

(recipe continues)

SHRIMP

1 teaspoon vegetable oil

1 pound jumbo (21/25) shell-on shrimp, peeled and deveined, shells reserved

1½ cups chicken stock, homemade (page 64) or store-bought

Zest of 1 lemon, cut into wide strips

2 ounces thick-cut smoky bacon (about 2 slices), diced

1 bunch scallions (white and tender green parts only), thinly sliced (about ¼ cup)

2 garlic cloves, finely chopped

2 tablespoons unsalted butter, at room temperature

1 tablespoon instant or all-purpose flour

Juice of 1 lemon (about 3 tablespoons)

Kosher salt and ground black pepper

Hot sauce

¼ cup coarsely chopped fresh flat-leaf parsley

4. Cook the bacon in the pot on **SAUTÉ MEDIUM** until crisp and rendered, about 8 minutes, stirring often. Add the scallions and garlic and cook until fragrant, about 30 seconds. Add the reserved stock and bring to a simmer.

5. Stir together the butter and flour in a small bowl until it forms a smooth paste and stir it into the pot. Cook until the liquid thickens to a sauce, about 3 minutes, stirring constantly.

6. Add the shrimp and cook only until opaque, about 2 minutes, stirring constantly. Stir in the lemon juice, then season with salt, pepper, and hot sauce. Serve straightaway over the grits, sprinkled with parsley.

VARIATION: Cheese Grits

Use a cheese of your choice that suits your tastes or pairs well with an accompanying dish. For example, Parmesan is subtle, extra-sharp white Cheddar is bold, and Gruyère is agreeably in the middle. In step 2 (in addition to the cream cheese) add 1 cup shredded cheese, 2 teaspoons hot sauce (or to taste), and 1 teaspoon garlic powder, and stir until smooth.

MULTICOOKER MULTITASKING

It is sometimes handy to have a second pot insert when preparing two or more dishes to serve together, so that you don't have to empty and wash the pot between recipes. Shrimp and Stoneground Grits is one of those times. With two pots, you can cook the grits in one, lift it out of the multicooker, and cover it to keep the grits warm while you prepare the shrimp in a second pot. A second pot would also be helpful with recipes served with Long-Grain Dinner Rice (page 41) or Really Good Mashed Potatoes (page 136).

Rice and Peas *in Parmesan Stock*

In the rice-growing regions of the South Carolina Lowcountry, this dish is sometimes called *risi e bisi* to reflect its Venetian roots. It's brothy enough to warrant a spoon, landing it somewhere between hearty soup and risotto. Petite green sweet peas are almost always better when purchased frozen unless they are picked and shelled right before they go into the pot.

PARMESAN STOCK

3 cups light-colored vegetable stock or chicken stock, homemade (pages 65 and 64) or store-bought

8 ounces Parmigiano-Reggiano rinds

8 large garlic cloves, chopped

1 dried bay leaf

Juice of 1 lemon (about 3 tablespoons)

RICE AND PEAS

3 tablespoons unsalted butter

½ cup finely chopped shallots

1 cup rinsed Arborio rice or unrinsed Carolina Gold rice

Kosher salt

2 cups fresh or thawed petite green peas (about 8 ounces)

½ cup finely grated Parmigiano-Reggiano cheese (about 1 ounce)

Finely grated zest and juice of 1 lemon (about 3 tablespoons)

2 tablespoons finely chopped fresh mint or chives

1. **For the stock:** Stir together the stock, cheese rinds, garlic, and bay leaf in the pot. Cover and cook on **HIGH PRESSURE** for 5 minutes. Let stand for **NATURAL RELEASE** for 5 minutes, then **QUICK RELEASE** the remaining pressure. Strain the stock into a bowl and set it aside until needed. Discard the solids (or nibble the rinds). Stir in the lemon juice.

2. **For the rice and peas:** Melt 2 tablespoons of the butter in the pot on **SAUTÉ MEDIUM**. Stir in the shallots and cook for 1 minute, stirring often. Add the rice and stir until coated in butter. Stir in the reserved Parmesan stock and 1 teaspoon salt. Cover and cook on **HIGH PRESSURE** for 4 minutes. Let stand for **NATURAL RELEASE** for 5 minutes, then **QUICK RELEASE** the remaining pressure.

3. Stir in the peas. The rice mixture should be hot enough to cook them, but if not, simmer on **SAUTÉ LOW** for 1 to 2 minutes. Do not overcook the peas; they should remain bright green.

4. Stir in the grated Parmigiano-Reggiano, lemon zest, lemon juice, and remaining 1 tablespoon butter. Taste and adjust the seasoning, if desired. Serve warm, sprinkled with mint.

Dirty Rice

The name of this hearty, well-seasoned dish comes from the browned bits of meat that flavor and speckle the white rice. One of the meats is finely chopped chicken liver, just enough to add great flavor and richness, akin to adding giblets to gravy. This is country cooking at its finest, with layers of nuanced flavor.

——— ∝⚬∝ ———

1½ cups long-grain white rice

2 teaspoons Creole seasoning

1 teaspoon unsalted butter

2 ounces thick-cut bacon (about 2 slices), diced

1 small yellow onion, finely chopped (about 1 cup)

1 medium green bell pepper, finely chopped (about 1 cup)

2 celery stalks, finely chopped (about ½ cup)

2 garlic cloves, finely chopped

1 jalapeño, finely chopped

Ground black pepper

4 ounces cleaned and finely chopped chicken or duck livers

4 ounces bulk breakfast sausage

¼ cup chopped fresh flat-leaf parsley

1 bunch scallions (white and tender greens parts only), thinly sliced (about ¼ cup)

——— ∝⚬∝ ———

> **HINT**
> *This recipe begins with freshly cooked rice, but it's a great way to use up left over rice too.*

1. Place the rice in a fine-mesh sieve and rinse thoroughly under cool running water to remove the surface starch. Pour the wet rice into the pot and stir in 1½ cups water, ½ teaspoon of the Creole seasoning, and the butter. Cover and cook on **HIGH PRESSURE** for 4 minutes. Let stand for **NATURAL RELEASE** for 10 minutes, then **QUICK RELEASE** the remaining pressure.

2. Pour the rice onto a rimmed baking sheet. Gently stir with a fork to loosen and fluff the grains. Spread in a single layer and set aside to cool to room temperature, stirring occasionally to speed cooling and break up any clumps.

3. Rinse and dry the pot to remove the sticky rice residue and return it to the multicooker. Cook the bacon on **SAUTÉ MEDIUM**, stirring often, until crisp and rendered, about 8 minutes. Use a slotted spoon to transfer the bacon to a bowl, leaving the fat in the pot.

4. Stir in the onion, bell pepper, and celery and cook until the mixture begins to soften, about 3 minutes, stirring often. Stir in the garlic, jalapeño, remaining 1½ teaspoons Creole seasoning, and ½ teaspoon black pepper. Cook for 1 minute while stirring. Stir in the chicken livers and sausage. Cook until the sausage is no longer pink, about 4 minutes, stirring often.

5. Reduce the heat to **SAUTÉ LOW**. Stir in the cooled rice and cook until warmed through, about 3 minutes. Add a splash of water if the rice begins to stick to the pot, but not so much that the rice turns mushy. Remove from the heat, stir in the parsley, scallions, and reserved bacon. Taste and adjust the seasoning, if desired. Serve hot.

Hoppin' John Risotto *with Collard Pesto*

Hoppin' John is a dish in which field peas and rice are served together. Hoppin' John and collard greens are often served on New Year's Day as a token for good luck and prosperity, with the peas and leafy greens symbolizing coins and folding money. Some traditions hold that the dish should include pork as well. There are many ways to prepare Hoppin' John, which makes the dish more of a common idea than a specific recipe. I prepare mine as a creamy risotto finished with a dollop of green pesto made with collard greens instead of basil. It's a wonderful combination, but the luckiest thing about this Hoppin' John is how easy it is to prepare perfect risotto in a multicooker.

Many people think that Hoppin' John must be made with black-eyed peas (see page 35), but that's not true. The earliest recipes for Hoppin' John used an heirloom variety of field peas called Sea Island Red Peas, which can be ordered online from Anson Mills. Most grocery stores sell a variety of fresh, frozen, and canned field peas, especially around New Year's Day—and you can use any of these in this Hoppin' John recipe. However, when using canned peas, which are already fully cooked and ready to use, be sure to take note of when they are added to the recipe to avoid overcooking them.

COLLARD PESTO

10 ounces small, tender, fresh collards, tough center ribs and stems discarded and leaves chopped

2 large garlic cloves, peeled

2 tablespoons finely chopped green olives or capers

2 tablespoons chopped oil-packed sun-dried tomatoes

¼ cup pecan pieces

¼ cup shredded Parmesan cheese (about 1 ounce)

1 tablespoon hot pepper vinegar or sherry vinegar

¾ cup extra-virgin olive oil, or as needed

½ teaspoon kosher salt

¼ teaspoon ground black pepper

Big pinch of cayenne pepper or red pepper flakes

RISOTTO

3 tablespoons unsalted butter

1 small yellow onion, finely diced (about 1 cup)

1 small red bell pepper, finely diced (about 1 cup)

2 celery stalks, finely diced (about ½ cup)

Kosher salt and ground black pepper

1 cup short-grain or risotto rice (such as Arborio or carnaroli) or Carolina Gold rice

½ cup dry white wine

3 cups chicken stock, homemade (page 64) or store-bought

1½ cups fresh, frozen, or canned field peas

8 ounces baked ham (such as Virginia ham), cut into small cubes (about 2 cups)

¼ cup shredded Parmesan cheese (about 1 ounce), plus more for serving

2 tablespoons finely chopped flat-leaf parsley

(recipe continues)

1. **For the collard pesto:** Pour 1½ cups water into the pot. Place the collards in a steamer basket and lower it into the pot. Cover and cook on **LOW PRESSURE** for 2 minutes. **QUICK RELEASE** the pressure. Lift out the basket and rinse the collards under cold running water until cool. Drain well.

2. Transfer the collards to a food processor and add the garlic, olives, sun-dried tomatoes, pecans, Parmesan, and vinegar and pulse until the mixture is finely chopped. With the machine running, add enough oil in a slow, steady stream to make a smooth, loose paste. Season with the salt, pepper, and cayenne. Serve at room temperature or refrigerate in an airtight container for up to 1 week.

3. **For the risotto:** Warm 2 tablespoons of the butter in the pot on **SAUTÉ MEDIUM**. Stir in the onion, bell pepper, celery, 2 teaspoons salt, and ½ teaspoon black pepper. Cook until the mixture begins to soften, about 3 minutes, stirring often.

4. Add the rice and stir to coat each grain in the butter. Cook until the outside of each grain is shiny and translucent with a tiny white dot in the center, about 2 minutes, stirring slowly and constantly.

5. Stir in the wine and cook until it evaporates, about 2 minutes. Stir in the stock. If using fresh or frozen field peas, stir them in now. If using canned, wait.

6. Cover and cook on **HIGH PRESSURE** for 5 minutes. Let stand for **NATURAL RELEASE** for 5 minutes, then **QUICK RELEASE** the remaining pressure. If using canned peas, add them now. Stir in the ham, Parmesan, parsley, and remaining 1 tablespoon butter. Taste and adjust the seasoning, if desired. Serve at once, topped with a sprinkling of Parmesan and a big spoonful of collard pesto.

Marinated Field Pea Relish

This versatile relish is usually served as a condiment or dip, similar to salsa. It's great served with chips or spooned over grilled meat and vegetables. It's also happy to sit, Texas-style, atop crisp saltine crackers.

---

8 ounces dried field peas

1 teaspoon Old Bay seasoning or kosher salt

4 garlic cloves, 2 smashed with the side of a knife and 2 finely chopped

3 large fresh flat-leaf parsley sprigs

1 cup bottled Italian dressing

1 (4-ounce) jar diced pimientos, drained

1 cup halved grape or cherry tomatoes

½ cup finely diced red bell pepper

1 jalapeño, finely chopped

¼ cup finely diced red onion

1 tablespoon hot sauce, or to taste

1 tablespoon Worcestershire sauce

½ cup finely chopped fresh flat-leaf parsley

---

1. Stir together the peas, 3 cups water, the Old Bay, smashed garlic, and parsley sprigs. Cover and cook on **HIGH PRESSURE** for 14 minutes. Let stand for **NATURAL RELEASE** for 15 minutes, then **QUICK RELEASE** the remaining pressure. Drain the peas and pour them into a large bowl. Stir in ¾ cup of the Italian dressing and let stand until cool, about 30 minutes.

2. Stir in the pimientos, tomatoes, bell pepper, jalapeño, onion, chopped garlic, hot sauce, Worcestershire, and chopped parsley. Moisten with more dressing, if needed. Cover and refrigerate for at least 4 hours and preferably overnight.

3. Before serving, return the relish to room temperature and stir well. Taste and adjust the seasoning, if desired. Refrigerate the salad in an airtight container for up to 1 week.

COOKING TIMES FOR DRIED BEANS AND PEAS

Dried beans and peas can eventually get so old and dried out that they will never turn tender and creamy, not even in a pressure cooker. Buy the freshest dried beans possible from a store that turns over inventory regularly, and don't let them disappear into the back of a cabinet.

When cooking beans in a multicooker, remember that you can always cook them more, but there's no remedy for overcooked beans. If the beans are still quite firm after the initial cooking, continue cooking them in 5-minute intervals under **HIGH PRESSURE**, followed by a **QUICK RELEASE**. If the beans are only slightly underdone, it is easier to simmer them (uncovered) on **SAUTÉ MEDIUM** until tender.

THERE'S MUCH MORE TO FIELD PEAS
THAN BLACK-EYED

Because dozens of different field pea varieties flourish in the South, most Southern grocery stores sell more than one type of field peas, and Southern farmers' markets and roadside produce stands can open up a trove of local specialties, such as Purple Hull, Pink-Eye, Crowder, Zipper, Whippoorwill, and Lady Cream (my personal favorite). Shop around and try field peas other than the ubiquitous black-eyed peas, which are not necessarily the tastiest.

Slow-Cooked Meaty Cowboy Beans

MAKES 4 TO 6 MAIN DISH SERVINGS OR 8 TO 10 SIDE DISH SERVINGS

This baked bean dish is sometimes known as campfire beans or barbecued baked beans. It makes a lot, which is just right for serving a crowd at a picnic, tailgate, or backyard gathering, although it's hearty enough to be a main dish. The recipe uses canned beans. Yes, one of the wonders of pressure-cooking is the ability to cook dried beans in minutes, but most Southern-style baked beans begin with canned beans that are doctored up to make them a homemade creation. During their low and slow simmer on the **SLOW COOKER** function, the beans have time to absorb the sauce's sweet and tangy seasoning, and the sauce has time to reduce and thickly coat the beans, just like beans simmered for hours over a campfire or baked in the oven.

4 ounces thick-cut smoky bacon (about 4 slices), diced

1½ pounds lean ground beef or bulk breakfast sausage

1 medium yellow onion, diced (about 1½ cups)

1 medium green bell pepper, diced (about 1 cup)

1 (15-ounce) can pork and beans, drained and rinsed

1 (15-ounce) can giant white lima beans or butter beans, drained and rinsed

1 (15-ounce) can kidney beans, drained and rinsed

1 (15-ounce) can pinto beans, drained and rinsed

1 cup thick, sweet, tomato-based barbecue sauce

½ cup packed dark brown sugar

½ cup apple cider vinegar, preferably unfiltered

1 tablespoon mustard powder

2 tablespoons finely chopped canned chipotles in adobe sauce (optional)

1. Cook the bacon in the pot on **SAUTÉ MEDIUM** until crisp and rendered, about 8 minutes, stirring often. Use a slotted spoon to transfer the bacon to a bowl, leaving the fat in the pot.

2. Stir in the ground beef, onion, and bell pepper. Cook until the beef is no longer pink, about 5 minutes, breaking up the meat with the spoon.

3. Stir in the beans, barbecue sauce, brown sugar, vinegar, and mustard powder. Stir in the chipotles for a little heat and smoky flavor, if desired. Cover and **SLOW COOK** on **LOW** for 8 hours, until thick and hot.

4. Just before serving, stir in the reserved bacon.

Red Beans and Rice

When a simple recipe calls for only a few ingredients, the caliber of those ingredients matters all the more. Red beans are a specific type of dried kidney bean, and many red bean experts swear by Camilla brand from New Orleans. Stovetop recipes often call for cooking the andouille sausage with the beans, but I find that the sausage becomes mealy and bland when cooked under pressure. Instead I cook the beans in the rendered sausage fat and save the sausage to stir in at the end, which results in fabulous flavor in record time.

2 tablespoons vegetable oil

1 pound andouille sausage, sliced into 1-inch-thick rounds

2 medium yellow onions, chopped (about 3 cups)

1 small green bell pepper, chopped (about 1 cup)

2 celery stalks, chopped (about ½ cup)

6 large garlic cloves, finely chopped

1 tablespoon dried basil

2 teaspoons Creole seasoning

½ teaspoon dried sage

½ teaspoon ground black pepper

3 dried bay leaves

1 pound dried red beans

Serve with: Long-Grain Dinner Rice (page 41), sliced scallions, chopped fresh flat-leaf parsley, and Crystal hot sauce

1. Warm the oil in the pot on **SAUTÉ MEDIUM**. Stir in the sausage and cook until browned, about 5 minutes, stirring often. Use a slotted spoon to transfer the sausage to a bowl, leaving the fat in the pot.

2. Stir in the onions, bell pepper, and celery. Cook until the mixture begins to soften, about 3 minutes.

3. Stir in the garlic, basil, Creole seasoning, sage, black pepper, and bay leaves. Cook until fragrant, about 1 minute, stirring constantly.

4. Stir in the beans and 4 cups water. Cover and cook on **HIGH PRESSURE** for 40 minutes. Let stand for **NATURAL RELEASE** for 20 minutes, then **QUICK RELEASE** the remaining pressure. If the beans are not tender, simmer them (uncovered) on **SAUTÉ MEDIUM** until they are, 5 to 10 minutes. Set the multicooker to **KEEP WARM**.

5. Vigorously stir the beans until the cooking liquid looks creamy. It's fine if you crush some of the beans. Stir in the reserved sausage and let stand for 10 minutes. Discard the bay leaves. Taste and adjust the seasoning, if desired.

6. Serve hot over rice and sprinkled with scallions and parsley, and hot sauce on the side.

ANDOUILLE SAUSAGE

Andouille is a coarse-grained, heavily smoked pork sausage that is highly seasoned with garlic and spices. High-quality, authentic andouille isn't always easy to find outside the Deep South or well-stocked charcuterie shops. Some of the processed commercial sausage labeled as andouille lacks the smoke, spice, and firmness of the real deal. If you cannot find good andouille, use the best and smokiest sausage you can find, perhaps kielbasa, Spanish chorizo, or a local specialty. If your sausage doesn't render a little tasty red fat, consider adding a big pinch of smoked paprika or ground chipotle chile to the dish.

Savannah Red Rice

This one-pot meal is exceptional in its ease and elegance, the dish that many experts lift up as the defining dish of the Georgia coast. It is essentially a hearty rice pilaf that is reminiscent of paella, in which seafood, smoky bacon, and long-grain rice simmer until plump and delectable.

1 teaspoon vegetable oil

1 pound extra-jumbo (16/20) shell-on shrimp, peeled and deveined, shells reserved

3 cups chicken stock, homemade (page 64) or store-bought

2 tablespoons apple cider vinegar, preferably unfiltered

2 ounces thick-cut smoky bacon (about 2 slices), diced

12 ounces andouille or similar spicy, smoked sausage, cut into ½-inch-thick rounds

1 medium onion, chopped (about 1½ cups)

2 celery stalks, chopped (about ½ cup)

2 garlic cloves, finely chopped

Kosher salt and ground black pepper

2 dried bay leaves

2 cups long-grain white rice (preferably Carolina Gold)

1¼ cups strained tomatoes (aka passata) or tomato sauce

2 tablespoons fresh thyme leaves

½ teaspoon red pepper flakes

1. Warm the oil in the pot on **SAUTÉ MEDIUM**. Add the shrimp shells and cook until they turn bright pink, about 2 minutes, stirring constantly. Pour in the chicken stock. Cover and cook on **HIGH PRESSURE** for 3 minutes. Let stand for **NATURAL RELEASE** for 5 minutes, then **QUICK RELEASE** the remaining pressure. Strain the stock into a large bowl (discard shells). Stir in the vinegar and set aside. Rinse and dry the pot.

2. Cook the bacon in the pot on **SAUTÉ MEDIUM** until crisp, about 8 minutes, stirring often. Add the sausage and cook, stirring occasionally, until browned, about 5 minutes. Transfer the bacon and sausage to a bowl, leaving the fat in the pot.

3. Add the onion and celery to the pot and cook until they start to soften, about 3 minutes. Stir in the garlic, 2 teaspoons salt, 1 teaspoon pepper, and the bay leaves and cook for 1 minute, stirring constantly.

4. Place the rice in a fine-mesh sieve and rinse under cool water to remove the surface starch. Stir the wet rice into the pot and cook for 1 minute, stirring to loosen the browned glaze from the bottom of the pot.

5. Stir in the reserved shrimp stock and strained tomatoes. Cover and cook on **HIGH PRESSURE** for 4 minutes. Let stand for **NATURAL RELEASE** for 10 minutes, then **QUICK RELEASE** the remaining pressure.

6. Fold in the shrimp, reserved sausage, and bacon. Continue folding until the shrimp turn opaque, about 2 minutes. Stir in thyme and pepper flakes. Discard the bay leaves; taste and adjust seasoning.

Long-Grain Dinner Rice

Freshly cooked long-grain white rice is such a daily staple in some Southern households that cooks put on a pot of rice and *then* decide what to make for dinner. White rice adds to the enjoyment of the dish without drawing undue attention, like background music played at just the right volume. A multicooker is an ideal rice cooker, capable of turning out great rice time after time, which is reassuring for those of us who have struggled with soggy stovetop rice. Perfect rice is a benchmark for some Southern recipes, and multicookers just turned us all into experts.

2 cups long-grain white rice

1 tablespoon unsalted butter

1 teaspoon kosher salt

1. Place the rice in a fine-mesh sieve and rinse thoroughly under cool running water to remove the surface starch. Pour the wet rice into the pot.

2. Stir in 2 cups water, the butter, and salt. Cover and cook on **HIGH PRESSURE** for 4 minutes. Let stand for **NATURAL RELEASE** for 10 minutes, then **QUICK RELEASE** the remaining pressure.

3. Gently stir with a fork to fluff the grains. Taste and adjust the seasoning, if desired.

Rise & Shine

Killed Lettuce with Poached Eggs
and Hot Bacon Vinaigrette

Salad for breakfast? Is that a thing? It is now, and what better on a breakfast salad than bacon and eggs? Where I'm from in the Blue Ridge Mountains, when a salad is dressed with a hot bacon vinaigrette it's usually called "killed" or "wilted" lettuce. The silky egg yolks mix with the vinegar in a way that always reminds me of the taste of béarnaise sauce. If you prefer semifirm yolks, cook them for 4 to 5 minutes; or for fully set yolks, cook them for 6 to 7 minutes. (See page 128 for more on cooking eggs in a multicooker.)

4 large eggs

8 cups lightly packed baby spinach, arugula, and/or sprightly spring leaf lettuces

2 spring onions or shallots, halved and thinly sliced (about ½ cup)

4 ounces thick-cut smoky bacon (about 4 slices), diced

6 tablespoons apple cider vinegar, preferably unfiltered

1 tablespoon sugar

Kosher salt and ground black pepper

1. Let the eggs sit at room temperature while preparing the other ingredients. Fill a large bowl with ice and water and set aside. Place the spinach and onions in a large salad bowl and have at the ready.

2. Cook the bacon in the pot on **SAUTÉ MEDIUM** until crisp and rendered, about 8 minutes, stirring often. Turn off the heat. Use a slotted spoon to transfer the bacon to a small bowl, leaving the fat in the pot.

3. Carefully add the vinegar and sugar to the hot bacon fat. It will sizzle vigorously at first. Working quickly, drizzle the hot vinaigrette over the spinach and onions, tossing with tongs to coat it lightly and evenly. Some of the spinach will wilt a bit, but it shouldn't be soggy. Divide among serving plates, season with salt and pepper, and let stand while preparing the eggs.

4. Rinse and dry the pot and return it to the multicooker. Pour 1 cup water into the pot. Place the eggs on an egg rack or in a steamer basket and lower them into the pot. Cover and cook on **LOW PRESSURE** for 3 minutes. **QUICK RELEASE** the pressure.

5. Immediately transfer the eggs to the ice water. Because you want to serve the eggs warm, remove them from the water as soon as they are cool enough to handle, no more than 2 minutes. Peel the eggs and place one on each salad. Sprinkle the reserved bacon over the salads and serve immediately.

Buttermilk Ricotta

One bite of fresh ricotta—warm or chilled—is persuasive evidence that it's worth the milk required to make it, at least once in a while as an indulgence. Fresh ricotta is so delicious that you can eat it with a spoon, but you should consider spreading warm ricotta on thick slabs of crunchy toast, drizzled with honey. Lightly chilled ricotta is also fabulous on toast, topped with avocado and/or tomato, drizzled with excellent olive oil, and finished with plenty of coarse salt and fresh pepper.

As the recipe title says, this recipe requires buttermilk. You can, of course, use this recipe to make regular ricotta with 12 cups of regular milk (what some Southerners once called sweet milk to distinguish it from pleasantly sour buttermilk), but without the healthful, natural cultures that are the defining trait of buttermilk, it won't be as tangy.

This recipe requires a multicooker with a YOGURT setting.

8 cups whole milk

4 cups whole buttermilk

Kosher salt

½ cup fresh lemon juice

1. Set a large, fine-mesh sieve over a large bowl and line it with a triple thickness of dampened cheesecloth, leaving a 3-inch overhang.

2. Stir together the milk, buttermilk, and 1 tablespoon salt in the pot. Cover, select the YOGURT function, and adjust to the BOIL setting. When the cooking time is complete (about 45 minutes), lift out the pot and set it on a trivet or towel on the counter.

3. Gently stir in the lemon juice. Let stand until the mixture separates into a thin, milky whey and very small white curds, about 10 minutes. Do not stir.

4. Ladle the curds and whey into the prepared sieve and let stand until the whey drains away, about 15 minutes. Lift the edges of the cheesecloth every few minutes to reposition the curds and encourage draining. When the draining slows to an occasional

(recipe continues)

HINT *Different styles and makes of multicookers have slightly different procedures for using the YOGURT function. To ensure you are following the proper procedure for your pot, consult your user manual, just in case it differs from what's written in this recipe.*

drip, gather all four corners of the cheesecloth and gently twist it into a bundle to compress the curds and press out any remaining whey. Taste the ricotta and add more salt, if desired.

5. Serve the ricotta while it is still a little warm, or let it cool to room temperature, cover tightly, and refrigerate until chilled. The ricotta will continue to firm as it cools and can be refrigerated for up to 1 week.

BUTTERMILK IS THE SOUTHERN DAIRY QUEEN

High-quality buttermilk contains the natural, good-for-us, probiotic cultures that are found in other fermented dairy products such as natural yogurt, kefir, and crème fraîche. The cultures once developed naturally in fresh milk that sat at room temperature for a few hours before it was churned to make butter. These days, most dairies make buttermilk by adding active cultures to pasteurized milk. Those cultures (plus acetic acid, lactic acid, and other things found in buttermilk) are what work culinary magic in many recipes, plus they give buttermilk its characteristic tang.

Buttermilk is plentiful and inexpensive in most places, especially across the South, and it keeps well for weeks. It's an easy, affordable luxury that makes a big difference in the success of recipes, so it's a shame that so many recipes and cooks suggest that one can replace liquid buttermilk with milk that's been curdled by vinegar or lemon juice. Other than being sour, there is no equivalence between cultured buttermilk and curdled milk. When buttermilk truly isn't available, replace it with another cultured dairy product, such as kefir or plain yogurt (with live, active cultures) that's thinned with a little milk to make it pourable.

Granola Porridge

Steel-cut oats, such as Scottish or Irish oats, are whole oats chopped into granular bits instead of rolled into flakes. They stay a bit chewy, even when fully cooked, which mitigates the gluey texture that some people don't like about standard oatmeal. A multicooker cuts the cooking time for steel-cut oats from about 1 hour to less than 10 minutes, and it eliminates presoaking, which means that making these hearty oats can be a quick fix on a busy morning. Stirring in a big handful of granola adds even more texture, intrigue, and flavor.

2 tablespoons unsalted butter

1 cup steel-cut Irish oats

1 cup whole milk or buttermilk

½ teaspoon kosher salt

1 cup granola

Serve with: butter, honey or sweet syrup (cane, maple, or sorghum), and flaky salt

1. Melt the butter in the pot on **SAUTÉ MEDIUM**. Stir in the oats and stir to coat. Cook for 1 minute while stirring.

2. Stir in the milk, 1 cup water, and salt. Cover and cook on **HIGH PRESSURE** for 8 minutes. Let stand for **NATURAL RELEASE** for 5 minutes, then **QUICK RELEASE** the remaining pressure.

3. Stir well. Fold in the granola and serve hot with a little extra butter, a drizzle of sweet syrup, and a pinch of flaky salt.

Hummingbird Coffee Cake
with Pineapple-Cream Cheese Glaze

Hummingbird Cake (a towering cream cheese–frosted layer cake made with tropical fruits like crushed pineapple and mashed bananas) originated as part of an advertising campaign to draw visitors to Jamaica. After a popular regional food magazine published the recipe in 1978, Hummingbird Cake fever spread across Southern kitchens, making it one of the most beloved cakes of all time. In this recipe, Hummingbird takes the form of a pineapple coffee cake. Moist and tender, this coffee cake is great for breakfast, or as a snack cake or dessert.

CAKE

Unsalted butter and flour
for the pan

1¾ cups all-purpose flour

¾ teaspoon baking powder

¼ teaspoon baking soda

½ teaspoon ground cinnamon

½ teaspoon kosher salt

8 tablespoons unsalted butter,
at room temperature

½ cup granulated sugar

2 large eggs, at room
temperature

1 teaspoon vanilla extract

1 cup mashed ripe banana
(about 1 small)

½ cup canned crushed
pineapple, drained and juice
reserved for the glaze

½ cup pecan pieces

1. **For the cake:** Butter and flour a 7-inch round baking pan. Whisk together the flour, baking powder, baking soda, cinnamon, and salt in a medium bowl and set aside.

2. In a stand mixer fitted with the paddle attachment (or in a large bowl if using a hand mixer), beat the butter and granulated sugar on high speed until light and fluffy, about 5 minutes.

3. Add the eggs one at a time, beating well and scraping down the sides of the bowl after each addition. Quickly beat in the vanilla, then add the banana, pineapple, and pecans and beat on low speed just until blended.

4. Add the flour mixture in two additions, beating on low speed just until smooth, and scraping down the sides and bottom of the bowl as needed. Transfer the batter to the prepared pan and cover tightly with aluminum foil.

5. Pour 2 cups water into the pot. Set the cake pan on a metal trivet with handles and lower them into the pot. Cover and cook on **HIGH PRESSURE** for 50 minutes. Let stand for **NATURAL RELEASE** for 10 minutes, then **QUICK RELEASE** the remaining pressure.

(recipe continues)

GLAZE

½ cup powdered sugar

½ cup cream cheese, at room temperature (4 ounces)

2 to 3 tablespoons pineapple juice

6. Uncover the cake and cool in the pan on the trivet for 20 minutes. Run a thin knife around the edges and turn out onto a serving plate.

7. **For the glaze:** Whisk together the powdered sugar and cream cheese in a small bowl until smooth. Add 2 to 3 tablespoons pineapple juice (reserved from the canned crushed pineapple) 1 tablespoon at a time, to make a thick glaze. Drizzle half of the glaze over the still-warm cake.

8. Let the cake cool to room temperature. Drizzle the remaining glaze over it and let stand until the glaze sets before slicing. Refrigerate leftovers in an airtight container for up to 3 days.

Country Ham *with Red-Eye Gravy*

Red-eye gravy is made by using strong black coffee to deglaze a skillet after frying slices of excellent, salt-cured, smoked, and aged country ham. It isn't common throughout the South, but it's dearly loved in some households, where it is traditionally served with grits (page 26), eggs, and biscuits. For a milder gravy, replace the coffee with brewed black tea or apple cider; inauthentic, yes, but it sure is tasty.

4 large slices country ham, sometimes called biscuit cuts (about 2 ounces each)

½ cup strong black coffee

1 to 2 tablespoons packed light brown sugar

Pinch of cayenne pepper, a good shake of hot sauce, or both

1. Lightly brown the ham on both sides in the pot on **SAUTÉ MEDIUM**, flipping with tongs, 1 to 2 minutes per side. Transfer to a plate. Turn off the heat to keep the browned glaze on the bottom of the pot from scorching.

2. Add the coffee and 1 tablespoon brown sugar to the pot and stir until the sugar dissolves.

3. Return the ham and any accumulated juices to the pot. Cover and cook on **HIGH PRESSURE** for 3 minutes. Let stand for **NATURAL RELEASE** for 5 minutes, then **QUICK RELEASE** the remaining pressure. Taste and add more brown sugar, if desired. Season with cayenne and serve piping hot.

Coconut Rice Pudding *with Ambrosia*

A multicooker works wonders with rice, including creamy rice pudding. The coconut milk in this recipe replaces the whole milk used in many traditional Southern recipes. Coconut is welcome in many forms on the Southern table, as is also seen in the ambrosia fruit salad, which makes a bright accompaniment to the creamy pudding. This recipe makes a fitting breakfast or brunch item, but no one will fuss if you serve it for dessert.

AMBROSIA

½ cup sweetened flaked coconut

½ cup chopped pecans

1 ruby red grapefruit

1 orange

½ pineapple, trimmed, cored, and cut into ½-inch cubes (about 2 cups)

PUDDING

1½ cups short-grain or risotto rice (such as Arborio or carnaroli)

½ teaspoon kosher salt

1 (13.5-ounce) can coconut milk, well stirred

2 large eggs

½ cup packed light brown sugar

1 teaspoon vanilla extract

1. **For the ambrosia:** Preheat the oven to 350°F.

2. Place the coconut and pecans on separate rimmed baking sheets and toast in the oven, shaking the pans once or twice, until the pecans are fragrant and the coconut is golden brown, 5 to 10 minutes. Immediately transfer each to separate plates to cool.

3. Use a sharp knife to cut just enough off the top and bottom of the grapefruit to expose the flesh. Sit the grapefruit cut-side down on a cutting board and slice off the peel and pith, following the curve of the fruit with the knife. Working over a large bowl, cut between the membranes to release grapefruit sections. Peel and section the orange the same way, adding it to the bowl with the grapefruit. Stir in the pineapple, coconut, and pecans.

4. **For the pudding:** Stir together 2½ cups water, the rice, and salt in the pot. Cover and cook on **HIGH PRESSURE** for 3 minutes. Let stand for **NATURAL RELEASE** for 10 minutes, then **QUICK RELEASE** the remaining pressure.

5. Meanwhile, whisk together the coconut milk, eggs, brown sugar, and vanilla in a medium bowl until smooth.

6. Stir about 1 cup of the hot rice into the coconut milk mixture to temper the eggs, then stir this mixture back into the pot. Cook on **SAUTÉ MEDIUM** until the pudding thickens to the consistency of cake batter, about 4 minutes, stirring slowly and constantly.

7. Spoon the rice pudding into serving bowls, top with ambrosia, and serve.

Ham and Cheese Bread Pudding
with Smoky Roasted Red Pepper Sauce

MAKES 6 SERVINGS

Most bread puddings must be refrigerated overnight, but this one can go into the multicooker after just 1 hour of soaking. With a generous layer of smoked ham and melty cheese in the middle, it tastes a bit like a warm, oversize breakfast sandwich. The roasted red pepper sauce is ready in about 5 minutes because it starts with the convenience of bottled marinara sauce. Finish the dish in the oven to brown the cheese on top.

BREAD PUDDING

Unsalted butter

4 large eggs

1 cup heavy cream

2 garlic cloves, finely chopped

2 teaspoons fresh thyme leaves

1 teaspoon kosher salt

1 teaspoon mustard powder

½ teaspoon smoked paprika

½ teaspoon ground black pepper

½ teaspoon freshly grated nutmeg

8 ounces country-style white bread or baguette, cut into 1-inch cubes (about 6 cups)

6 ounces Black Forest ham, chopped

1 cup shredded Asiago or Italian blend cheese (about 4 ounces)

¼ cup shredded Parmesan cheese (about 1 ounce)

1. **For the bread pudding:** Butter a 1½-quart round baking dish. Whisk together the eggs, cream, garlic, thyme, salt, mustard powder, paprika, pepper, and nutmeg in a large bowl. Stir in the bread. Let stand 10 minutes, stirring occasionally.

2. Spoon half of the bread mixture into the baking dish. Add the ham and Asiago cheese in an even layer. Top with the rest of the bread mixture and drizzle with any remaining liquid. Cover tightly with aluminum foil. Refrigerate for at least 1 hour or up to overnight.

3. Pour 1½ cups water into the pot. Set the covered baking dish on a metal trivet with handles and lower them into the pot. Cover and cook on **HIGH PRESSURE** for 25 minutes. Let stand for **NATURAL RELEASE** for 20 minutes, then **QUICK RELEASE** the remaining pressure. Remove the dish, uncover, and sprinkle with Parmesan.

4. Position an oven rack 5 inches from the heat source and heat the broiler. Broil the bread pudding until the cheese melts and browns, about 2 minutes. Set aside.

SAUCE

⎯⎯⎯∞⎯⎯⎯

1½ cups bottled marinara sauce

½ cup drained and finely chopped roasted red peppers

1 tablespoon sherry vinegar

1 teaspoon packed light brown sugar

1 teaspoon smoked paprika

5. **For the sauce:** Empty and dry the pot and return it to the multi-cooker. Stir together the marinara, red peppers, sherry vinegar, brown sugar, and smoked paprika in the pot. Cook on SAUTÉ LOW until warmed, about 3 minutes. (Alternatively, warm the sauce in a small saucepan over medium heat.)

6. Serve the bread pudding warm, topped with a spoonful of the warm sauce.

Hearty Soups, Stews & a Gumbo

Zesty Black Bean Soup *with Lime Cream*

Homemade black bean soup is filling, satisfying, nutritious, and thanks to a multicooker, faster than ever. Who could have imagined a way to cook dried beans in minutes with no need for an overnight soak? This soup relies on using high-impact ingredients that quickly build flavor, such as a generous amount of dried herbs and spices, fresh lime, and salsa verde. The pomegranate arils on top are uncommon, but their sweet-tart flavor and juicy crunch are tasty, and pretty, too.

SOUP

1 pound dried black beans

6 cups vegetable stock or chicken stock, homemade (pages 65 and 64) or store-bought

Juice of 2 limes (about ¼ cup)

1 tablespoon garlic powder

1 tablespoon onion powder

2 teaspoons ground cumin

2 teaspoon dried Mexican oregano

2 teaspoons kosher salt

1 cup bottled spicy salsa verde

LIME CREAM

1½ cups sour cream

Finely grated zest and juice of 1 lime (about 2 tablespoons)

1 tablespoon green hot sauce, or to taste

Kosher salt

Serve with: lime wedges, sliced fresh avocado, pomegranate arils, green hot sauce, and/or tortilla chips

1. **For the soup:** Stir together the beans, stock, lime juice, garlic powder, onion powder, cumin, oregano, and salt in the pot. Cover and cook on **HIGH PRESSURE** for 30 minutes. Let stand for **NATURAL RELEASE** of the pressure. If the beans are not as tender as you like, simmer the soup on **SAUTÉ MEDIUM** for 5 to 10 minutes, stirring occasionally.

2. Stir in the salsa verde. Taste and adjust the seasoning, if desired. For thicker soup, puree about half of it with an immersion blender directly in the pot. (Or purée about half of the soup in a stand blender and return it to the pot.)

3. **For the lime cream:** Stir together the sour cream, lime zest, lime juice, and hot sauce. Season with salt. Serve the soup warm, with lime wedges, avocado, pomegranate arils, hot sauce, and chips.

> HINT *When you need pretty, bright green zest, choose a bright green lime. But when seeking lots of juice, choose a lime that is softer and paler. (A 20-second zap in the microwave helps, too.)*

Beef Stew in Great Gravy

It's the little things that elevate a good beef stew to a great one. Skip packages of so-called "stew beef" and start with an economical chuck roast that you can cut into large chunks. Stew beef isn't bad meat, but it's a mismatched assortment of trimmings from all sorts of cuts that won't cook up the same way or finish at the same time. I use canned beef consommé in this recipe because it contains a little gelatin that adds body to the gravy. Worcestershire and soy sauce add the deep, satisfying savory taste known as umami.

4-pound chuck roast

Kosher salt and ground black pepper

2 tablespoons vegetable oil, or more as needed

1 cup dry red wine

1½ cups beef consommé, beef stock, or chicken stock (homemade, page 64, or store-bought)

¼ cup tomato paste

2 tablespoons Worcestershire sauce

2 tablespoons soy sauce

1 medium yellow onion, peeled and halved

3 large garlic cloves, chopped

2 dried bay leaves

2 small fresh rosemary sprigs

2 large fresh thyme sprigs

2 pounds fingerling potatoes, halved lengthwise, or quartered new potatoes

6 medium carrots (about 1 pound), peeled and cut into 2-inch lengths

1. Trim the roast well, cutting off and discarding any big pieces of fat. Cut the chuck into 4-inch pieces, blot dry with paper towels, and season with 2 teaspoons salt and 1 teaspoon pepper.

2. Warm the oil in the pot on **SAUTÉ HIGH**. Working in batches to not crowd the meat, cook the meat until deeply browned on all sides, turning the meat with tongs, 3 to 4 minutes per side, then transfer to a large bowl. Add more oil to the pot if needed between batches. If the browned glaze on the bottom of the pot begins to scorch, reduce the heat to **SAUTÉ MEDIUM**.

3. Add the wine and stir to loosen any browned bits on the bottom of the pot. (You might get a burn warning message if there are solids stuck to the bottom of the pot during pressure-cooking.) Simmer until reduced by half, about 5 minutes.

4. Stir in the consommé, tomato paste, Worcestershire, and soy sauce. Return the meat and any accumulated juices to the pot with the halved onion, garlic, bay leaves, rosemary, and thyme.

5. Cover and cook on **HIGH PRESSURE** for 30 minutes. Let stand for **NATURAL RELEASE** for 20 minutes, then **QUICK RELEASE** the remaining pressure. Discard the halved onion, bay leaves, and herb stems.

4 medium parsnips
(about 8 ounces), peeled and cut
into 2-inch pieces

2 cups frozen or peeled fresh
pearl onions (about 8 ounces)

1 cup frozen peas
(about 4 ounces)

3 tablespoons cornstarch,
plus more as needed

————⧓————

6. Add the potatoes, carrots, parsnips, and pearl onions. Cover and cook on **HIGH PRESSURE** for 10 minutes. **QUICK RELEASE** the pressure. Stir in the peas and taste and adjust the seasoning, if desired.

7. Ladle about 1 cup of the liquid into a small bowl and whisk in the cornstarch until smooth. Stir this slurry into the pot and cook on **SAUTÉ MEDIUM** until the gravy thickens, about 2 minutes. If you prefer thicker gravy, repeat the process with another 1 to 2 tablespoons of cornstarch. Serve warm.

Chicken Stock

Rich, homemade chicken stock that tastes like chicken is among the most amazing things we can make in a multicooker. It is so full of body that it congeals when refrigerated and it's ready in an hour instead of an afternoon. Pressure-cooking to make this stock leaves any chicken meat no longer palatable, so use inexpensive bony pieces that make tastier stock. The liquid inside a sealed multicooker doesn't evaporate, plus the pressure draws out the chicken juices, so it yields more stock than the amount of water used in the recipe.

———— ∽ ————

3 to 4 pounds bony chicken parts, such as wings, drumettes, backs, and necks

2 medium yellow onions, coarsely chopped (about 3 cups)

2 large carrots, cut into chunks (about 2 cups)

2 celery stalks, cut into chunks (about ½ cup)

6 large fresh flat-leaf parsley sprigs

3 large fresh thyme sprigs

2 tablespoons distilled white or apple cider vinegar

1 dried bay leaf

1 tablespoon kosher salt

1 teaspoon black peppercorns

———— ∽ ————

1. Place the chicken parts, onions, carrots, celery, parsley, thyme, vinegar, bay leaf, salt, and peppercorns in the pot.

2. Add water to cover (about 2 quarts), taking care not to fill the pot more than two-thirds full. Cover and cook on **HIGH PRESSURE** for 1 hour. Let stand for **NATURAL RELEASE** of the pressure.

3. Strain the stock through a fine-mesh sieve and discard the solids. If not using the stock immediately, quickly cool it to room temperature by sitting the bowl in an ice bath. Transfer the cooled stock to airtight containers and refrigerate for up to 5 days or freeze for up to 6 months.

HINT *When freezing stock, divide it into the portion size you use most often in recipes (such as 1, 2, or 4 cups) to avoid having to thaw more at once than you need. Be sure to leave plenty of headspace in the containers to accommodate the expansion of the liquid when it freezes.*

Golden Vegetable Stock

This pale stock won't stain light-colored recipes and tastes great in any recipe that calls for vegetable stock. The vegetables don't have to be in peak form, but they shouldn't be a shriveled mess with no more flavors to give. You can include vegetable peels and trimmings left over from other recipes (I like to accumulate them in an airtight container or zip-top bag that I stash in the freezer until I'm ready to make stock.) Don't include dark red or green vegetables that will darken the stock, or cruciferous vegetables (such as broccoli), which will make it bitter.

3 medium yellow onions, quartered (about 5 cups)

4 large carrots, scrubbed and cut into large chunks (about 4 cups)

4 celery stalks, cut into large chunks (about 1 cup)

2 leeks (white and light-green parts only), sliced (about 2 cups)

8 garlic cloves, halved

8 large fresh thyme sprigs

8 large fresh parsley sprigs

1 dried bay leaf

1 teaspoon kosher salt

1 teaspoon black peppercorns

½ teaspoon allspice berries

½ teaspoon yellow mustard seeds

1 tablespoon white wine vinegar

¼ teaspoon tumeric (optional)

1. Place the onions, carrots, celery, leeks, garlic, thyme, parsley, bay leaf, salt, peppercorns, allspice berries, and mustard seeds in the pot. Add water to cover (about 2 quarts). Cover and cook on **HIGH PRESSURE** for 30 minutes. Let stand for **NATURAL RELEASE** of the pressure.

2. Strain through a fine-mesh sieve into a large bowl, pressing firmly on the solids to extract as much liquid as possible. Stir in the vinegar. Stir in turmeric for color, if desired.

3. If not using the stock immediately, quickly cool it to room temperature by sitting the bowl in an ice bath. Transfer the cooled stock to airtight containers and refrigerate for up to 5 days or freeze for up to 6 months.

Tomato and Peanut Soup

Mafé, a peanut or groundnut stew from Senegal, is my inspiration for this recipe. The combination of spice, peanuts, and tomatoes is among many examples of the contributions of West African cooks whose resourceful expertise with flavors, ingredients, and techniques formed a cornerstone of what we now call Southern food.

SOUP

2 tablespoons unsalted butter

1 medium yellow onion, finely diced (about 1½ cups)

2 celery stalks, finely diced (about ½ cup)

2 tablespoons tomato paste

1 tablespoon packed dark brown sugar

1 teaspoon kosher salt

1 teaspoon Old Bay seasoning

1 teaspoon red curry powder

¼ teaspoon cayenne pepper

2 small sweet potatoes, peeled and cut into ½-inch cubes (about 3 cups)

2 (14.5-ounce) cans diced fire-roasted tomatoes with their juices

2 cups vegetable stock or chicken stock, homemade (pages 65 and 64) or store-bought

½ cup smooth all-natural peanut butter

½ cup half-and-half or well-stirred coconut milk

TOPPING

2 cups halved cherry tomatoes

1 cup salted roasted peanuts

2 bunches scallions (white and tender green parts only), thinly sliced (about ½ cup)

Kosher salt and ground black pepper

> HINT *Red curry powder is an aromatic spice blend made with coriander, cumin, clove, nutmeg, cardamom, and mild ground chiles. It is available in most grocery stores and spice shops, and online. When red curry powder isn't available, replace it with a similar Indian spice blend.*

1. **For the soup:** Melt the butter in the pot on **SAUTÉ MEDIUM**. Stir in the onion and celery and cook until tender, about 5 minutes. Stir in the tomato paste, brown sugar, salt, Old Bay, red curry powder, and cayenne and cook 1 minute, stirring constantly. Stir in the sweet potatoes, tomatoes, stock, and peanut butter. Cover and cook on **HIGH PRESSURE** for 10 minutes. Let stand for **NATURAL RELEASE** for 10 minutes, then **QUICK RELEASE** the remaining pressure.

2. Stir in the half-and-half. Taste and adjust the seasoning, if desired. Let stand while preparing the topping.

3. **For the topping:** Toss together the cherry tomatoes, peanuts, and scallions in a small bowl. Season with salt and pepper. To serve, ladle soup into shallow serving bowls. Spoon the cherry tomato mixture on top and serve.

Velvety Potato and Leek Soup

You can make this creamy, comforting soup in about half an hour in a multicooker, including pureeing it directly in the pot with an immersion blender. It's refined and elegant, although you can take it in a casual direction by topping it as though it were a loaded baked potato, with items such as shredded cheese, chopped scallions, crisp bacon, chives, and a dollop of sour cream. You could also add cooked broccoli or asparagus tips. This versatile recipe can serve as a framework for other root vegetable soups if you replace up to half of the potato with other starchy vegetables, such as turnips, rutabagas, or Jerusalem artichokes. And although cauliflower is not a starchy vegetable, you can use it with a little extra potato to help with body and texture.

4 tablespoons unsalted butter

3 medium leeks
(white and tender green parts
only) or 2 medium yellow onions,
chopped (about 3 cups)

2 pounds russet potatoes,
peeled and diced
(about 6 cups)

4 cups chicken stock or light-
colored (see Hint) vegetable
stock, homemade (pages 64 and
65) or store-bought

1 teaspoon celery seeds

½ teaspoon mustard powder

¼ teaspoon freshly
grated nutmeg

Kosher salt and ground
black pepper

1 cup crème fraîche (homemade,
page 141, or store-bought)
or heavy cream

1. Melt the butter in the pot on **SAUTÉ MEDIUM**. Stir in the leeks and cook until they begin to soften, about 3 minutes.

2. Stir in the potatoes, stock, celery seeds, mustard powder, nutmeg, 2 teaspoons salt, and ¼ teaspoon black pepper. Cover and cook on **HIGH PRESSURE** for 5 minutes. Let stand for **NATURAL RELEASE** for 15 minutes, then **QUICK RELEASE** the remaining pressure.

3. Purée with an immersion blender directly in the pot. (Alternatively, puree the soup in batches in a stand blender, filling it no more than half full with hot liquid. Return the soup to the pot.)

4. Stir in the crème fraîche. Taste and adjust the seasoning, if desired. Serve warm.

> HINT *When using store-bought vegetable stock to make this soup vegetarian, select a light-colored stock that doesn't contain tomatoes as its first ingredient to avoid turning the soup ruddy. This type of meatless stock is meant to resemble chicken stock, so it is often called something like no-chick'n broth.*

Frito Pie

The classic combo of chili and chips is sometimes called Frito Pie when individual bags of chips are split open to hold the chili and toppings. While the chili is just as tasty when served in bowls, it's perhaps not as much fun. I use finely ground cornmeal to thicken the chili just before serving to ensure it isn't too soupy when it's ladled into the bags of chips (when serving the chili in a bowl, you can skip the thickening if you prefer). Ground ancho chile is mild and fruity, and chipotle is smoky and packs some heat. No matter the spice level, a little unsweetened cocoa enhances the ground chiles, but there's not so much that the chili tastes chocolaty. Dried Mexican oregano is stronger and less sweet than Mediterranean or Greek oregano, and pairs well with chiles and cumin.

1 tablespoon vegetable oil

1½ pounds ground chuck or ground dark-meat turkey

2 medium yellow onions, chopped (about 3 cups)

1 teaspoon kosher salt, plus more to taste

½ cup tomato paste

2 garlic cloves, finely chopped

2 tablespoons ground dried chiles, such as ancho, chipotle, or a combination

2 teaspoons unsweetened cocoa powder

1 teaspoon ground cumin

1 teaspoon dried oregano (preferably Mexican oregano)

1 cup dark beer

1 cup beef stock

1 (14.5-ounce) petite diced tomatoes with their liquid

3 cups cooked or canned black or pinto beans (drained and rinsed, if canned)

2 tablespoons masa harina or fine cornmeal (optional)

8 individual packages or 1 large bag of corn chips, preferably Fritos

Juice of 2 limes (about ¼ cup)

Serve with: shredded Monterey Jack or Mexican blend cheese, sour cream, and pickled jalapeños

1. Warm the oil in the pot on **SAUTÉ MEDIUM**. Stir in the ground meat and cook until no longer pink, about 5 minutes, stirring to break it up. Add the onions and salt. Stir to coat in the drippings. Cook until the onions begin to soften, about 3 minutes, stirring occasionally.

2. Stir in the tomato paste, garlic, ground chile, cocoa powder, cumin, and oregano, and cook for 1 minute, stirring constantly. Reduce the heat if the spices start to stick or scorch.

(recipe continues)

3. Add the beer and beef stock, and stir to loosen every speck of the browned bits and glaze from the bottom of the pot. Cover and cook on **HIGH PRESSURE** for 10 minutes. Let stand for **NATURAL RELEASE** for 20 minutes, and then **QUICK RELEASE** the remaining pressure.

4. Stir in the tomatoes and beans, and simmer uncovered on **SAUTÉ MEDIUM** for 10 minutes. If you prefer thicker chili, ladle about 1 cup of the liquid into a small bowl, whisk in the masa until smooth, and stir it into the pot. Cook until thickened, about 1 minute, stirring slowly and constantly. Taste and adjust the seasoning, if desired.

5. To serve, split open the bags of Fritos to create bowls of sorts (or divide the large bag of chips among serving bowls). Stir the lime juice into the chili, then spoon it over the chips. Top with cheese, sour cream, and jalapeños and serve at once.

KEEPING DRIED HERBS FRESH

Dried herbs and spices last about 1 year once opened, or less time if they are exposed to excessive heat and humidity. (Store them in a cabinet or pantry away from the stove.) Give your spices a sniff test from time to time. The bold, pungent aroma should bowl you over. If their aroma has faded away, so has their flavor, and they are adding little more than dust to your recipes.

Winter Squash Soup
with Apple Butter Cream

MAKES ABOUT 2 QUARTS

Every cook needs at least one great winter squash soup in their repertoire. The most familiar winter squash is probably butternut, but there are many choices worth exploring, including heirloom varieties and cooking pumpkins. Take a closer look at the offerings at the grocery store and farmers' markets, especially during fall and winter. The colorful squashes and pumpkins might look like holiday decorations, but if they are in the produce department, they're meant to be eaten. Some of my favorite butternut alternatives are red kuri, kabocha, and sugar pumpkins. Broadly speaking, the flesh of all edible winter squashes and pumpkins can be used interchangeably—and a multicooker can make them easier to peel and then tender enough to puree in only minutes.

SOUP

3 tablespoons unsalted butter

2 medium leeks (white and tender green parts only), halved and thinly sliced (about 1 cup)

2 medium carrots, chopped (about 1 cup)

1 celery stalk, chopped (about ¼ cup)

1 teaspoon kosher salt

1 teaspoon garam masala

½ teaspoon ground ginger

½ teaspoon ground coriander

2 cups chicken stock or vegetable stock, homemade (pages 64 and 65) or store-bought

1 small winter squash or pie pumpkin (about 2 pounds), peeled, seeded, and cut into 1-inch pieces (about 6 cups)

1. **For the soup:** Melt the butter in the pot on **SAUTÉ MEDIUM**. Stir in the leeks, carrots, celery, and salt. Cook until beginning to soften, about 3 minutes, stirring often. Stir in the garam masala, ginger, and coriander and cook for 1 minute, stirring constantly.

2. Pour in the stock and stir to loosen any glaze from the bottom of the pot. Stir in the squash, apple, and thyme sprig. Cover and cook on **HIGH PRESSURE** for 8 minutes. Let stand for **NATURAL RELEASE** for 15 minutes, then **QUICK RELEASE** the remaining pressure. Discard the thyme stem. Stir in the apple cider and maple syrup.

3. Puree the soup with an immersion blender directly in the pot. (Alternatively, puree the soup in batches in a stand blender, filling the blender no more than half full with hot liquid. Return the soup to the pot.) Taste and adjust the seasoning, if desired. Turn off the heat and let the soup cool while preparing the cream. This soup tastes best when served barely warm.

72 - *Instantly* Southern

1 tart apple (such as Pink Lady),
peeled, cored, and diced

1 large fresh thyme sprig

1 cup unsweetened apple cider,
preferably unfiltered

2 tablespoons maple syrup or
packed dark brown sugar,
or to taste

APPLE BUTTER CREAM

1 cup crème fraîche (homemade,
page 141, or store-bought)
or sour cream

¼ cup apple butter

Pinch of kosher salt

HINT
*Garam masala is a blend of
warm, gentle, aromatic ground
spices such as cinnamon,
mace, allspice, and cardamom.
It's easy to find in most well-
stocked grocery stores and
spice shops, but if not, replace it
with pumpkin pie spice and
a pinch of cayenne.*

---

4. **For the apple butter cream:** Whisk together the crème fraîche and apple butter in a small bowl. Season with the salt.

5. To serve: Ladle the soup into serving bowls and top with a dollop of apple butter cream.

PREP TIPS FOR WINTER SQUASH

Some winter squashes can be as hard as rocks and a challenge to peel and chop. You can partially cook the squash in the multicooker to soften their skins, or fully cook the squash if you plan to puree it in a recipe, such as this one. Pour 1½ cups water into the pot. Sit the squash on a metal trivet with handles and lower it into the pot. (If the squash is too large to slide into the pot, snap off the stem and/or cut it in half.) Cook on **HIGH PRESSURE** from 5 minutes (to soften just enough to peel more easily) to 12 minutes (to soften enough to fully cook the squash), then **QUICK RELEASE** the pressure. The cooking time depends on the size of the squash and how soft you want the flesh. For example, a 2-pound butternut will be tender enough to peel and cube in 5 minutes and soft enough to mash in 8 minutes. If you aren't certain about the likely cooking time, start with a shorter time and then test for doneness by piercing the squash with a knife. If it's not as tender as you need, cook on **HIGH PRESSURE** for a couple more minutes, again followed by a **QUICK RELEASE**. Remove it from the pot and let stand until cool enough to handle.

Yakamein

Yakamein is a beef and noodle soup similar to ramen. It's beloved in New Orleans, likely brought there by Chinese immigrants in the nineteenth century where it became of a fusion of Asian and local ingredients. One will find both haute and humble versions of the dish across the city, from fancy restaurants to food trucks to vendor carts at outdoor festivals. No matter the source, yakamein hits the spot in ways that are difficult to articulate, and are better tasted than told. It's salty, spicy, filling, and reassuring—just the thing that some people crave when trying to manage a hangover or fill an empty belly after a night of revelry in New Orleans, which is why yakamein is sometimes nicknamed Old Sober.

4 pounds chuck roast

1 teaspoon kosher salt, or to taste

2 quarts beef stock

½ cup soy sauce

1 tablespoon Worcestershire sauce

2 teaspoons Creole seasoning

1 pound spaghetti

4 large hard-cooked eggs (see page 128), peeled and halved

2 bunches scallions (white and tender green parts only), thinly sliced (about ½ cup)

Serve with: soy sauce, Worcestershire sauce, and hot sauce

1. Trim the roast well and discard any big pieces of fat. Cut the meat into 4-inch pieces, blot them dry with paper towels, season with salt, and place in the pot.

2. Add the beef stock, soy sauce, Worcestershire, and Creole seasoning and push the meat down to ensure it is fully submerged in the liquid. Cover and cook on **HIGH PRESSURE** for 45 minutes. Let stand for **NATURAL RELEASE** for 15 minutes, then **QUICK RELEASE** the remaining pressure.

3. Use a spider or slotted spoon to transfer the meat to a bowl. When it has cooled slightly, use tongs or two forks to shred the meat and set aside.

4. Add the spaghetti to the pot; only about half of it will be submerged. Let stand for a minute or so until the submerged part softens enough to bend, then use a spoon to push all of the spaghetti into the liquid.

5. Cover and cook on **HIGH PRESSURE** for 8 minutes. **QUICK RELEASE** the pressure. Taste and adjust the seasoning, if desired.

6. To serve, divide the soup among shallow serving bowls. Top each with shredded meat, one egg half, and scallions. Serve with soy sauce, Worcestershire sauce, and hot sauce.

Chicken and Sausage Gumbo

Despite its daunting reputation, roux is nothing more than flour and fat cooked together until they transform into a smooth paste that can thicken a recipe. Roux cooked until it is dark adds flavor in addition to thickening power, and is a building block of Cajun and Creole cuisine, including gumbo. There's no rushing a dark roux. It requires several minutes of attentive stirring, whether prepared in a multicooker or on the stovetop. (Although there is an alternative if you have access to an oven. See Oven-Baked Roux, opposite.) To make the most of your time, prepare the roux before chopping or prepping any other ingredients, so that it will reach a stage where you no longer must stir nonstop, and it will continue to darken slightly while you work on other parts of the recipe. Once everything is in the multicooker, this gumbo is ready to serve in minutes.

ROUX

½ cup peanut oil or vegetable oil

½ cup all-purpose flour

GUMBO

1 medium yellow onion, chopped (about 1½ cups)

1 medium green bell pepper, chopped (about 1½ cups)

2 celery stalks, chopped (about ½ cup)

4 garlic cloves, chopped

1 tablespoon Creole seasoning

1 tablespoon Worcestershire sauce

4 cups chicken stock, homemade (page 64) or store-bought

1 pound boneless, skinless chicken thighs, cut into 2-inch pieces

12 ounces andouille sausage, cut into ½-inch-thick rounds

1. **For the roux:** Stir together the peanut oil and flour in the pot until smooth. Cook on **SAUTÉ MEDIUM** until the roux is the color of peanut butter, about 25 minutes, stirring constantly with a wooden spoon or heatproof spatula.

2. Set the pot to **WARM HIGH**. Let the roux stand while you chop and prep the gumbo ingredients, stirring occasionally. It will continue to darken slightly.

3. **For the gumbo:** When you are ready to finish the recipe, warm the roux on **SAUTÉ MEDIUM** until it begins to bubble, stirring constantly.

4. Stir in the onion, bell pepper, and celery and cook until they begin to soften, about 3 minutes. Stir in the garlic, Creole seasoning, and Worcestershire and cook for 1 minute.

5. Stir in the chicken stock, then stir in the chicken and andouille. Cover and cook on **HIGH PRESSURE** for 8 minutes. Let stand for **NATURAL RELEASE** for 2 minutes, then **QUICK RELEASE** the remaining pressure.

3 cups (12 ounces) fresh
or frozen okra, cut into
½-inch-thick rounds

1 pound medium
(26/30) shrimp, peeled and
deveined

———— ∞ ————

Serve with: Long-Grain Dinner Rice
(page 41)

6. Stir in the okra and let stand on **KEEP WARM** until it is tender, about 5 minutes, stirring occasionally. (The stew will be hot enough to cook it.)

7. Add the shrimp and stir gently until they turn opaque, about 2 minutes. Taste and adjust the seasoning, if desired. Serve warm over the rice.

VARIATION: Oven-Baked Roux   MAKES ABOUT 1 CUP

You can bake the roux to eliminate the many minutes of constant stirring in the pot. This method makes twice as much roux as you need for the gumbo recipe, but you can store the other half in the freezer to use the next time you make gumbo.

———— ∞ ————

1 cup peanut oil or vegetable oil

1 cup all-purpose flour

———— ∞ ————

1. Preheat the oven to 350°F.

2. Whisk together the oil and flour until smooth in a small cast-iron skillet or heavy baking pan. Bake until the roux reaches the color of peanut butter, about 45 minutes, stirring every 15 minutes to keep it from scorching around the edge. For dark roux, continue baking and stirring every 15 minutes until it reaches the desired shade of brown. The darker the roux, the deeper the flavor, but the less its thickening power.

3. If you are using the roux immediately in the gumbo, carefully pour it into the pot and proceed with step 3. If making the roux ahead, transfer it into a heatproof bowl to cool to room temperature. Store it in airtight container in the refrigerator for up to 1 week or freeze for up to 3 months. When it's time to use the roux, melt and heat it in the pot as described in step 3 of the gumbo recipe.

Texas Bowl of Red

Purists insist that true chili is chock-full of cubed (not ground) beef that's richly seasoned with red chiles, with no beans in sight. The beef in a bowl of red is braised, a task that a multicooker does rapidly and well, turning a tough (but tasty) chuck roast spoon-tender with only 30 minutes of pressure-cooking, a fraction of the time required on a stovetop. Try to use at least two of the chile varieties listed in the ingredient list and toast them in the pot to create a deep, robust flavor base for the dish. Packages of whole dried chiles are available in well-stocked grocery stores and neighborhood tiendas, and some markets sell the chiles threaded onto lengths of string.

2 ounces dried whole New Mexico, guajillo, and/or pasilla chiles

2 cups beef stock

1 (14.5-ounce) can diced fire-roasted tomatoes with their juices

1 canned chipotle chile in adobo sauce, plus 2 teaspoons of the adobo sauce

4 pounds beef chuck roast, fat trimmed away, cut into 1½-inch pieces

2 teaspoons kosher salt

1½ teaspoons ground black pepper

1 tablespoon vegetable oil, plus more as needed

1 medium yellow onion, finely chopped (about 1½ cups)

2 garlic cloves, finely chopped

2 teaspoons ground cumin

½ teaspoon ground cinnamon

1. Discard the stems and seeds from the chiles. Toast the chiles in the pot on **SAUTÉ HIGH** until fragrant and lightly browned in spots on both sides, turning with tongs, 5 to 7 minutes.

2. Add the beef stock and 1 cup water. Cover and cook on **HIGH PRESSURE** for 10 minutes. **QUICK RELEASE** the pressure.

3. Strain the chiles through a fine-mesh sieve set over a bowl. Reserve the cooking liquid.

4. Transfer the chiles to a blender. Add the canned tomatoes, chipotle chile, adobo sauce, and 2 tablespoons of the reserved cooking liquid. Blend to a smooth paste and set aside.

5. Rinse and dry the pot and return it to the multicooker.

6. Blot the beef chunks dry with paper towels and season with the salt and pepper.

7. Warm 1 tablespoon of the oil in the pot on **SAUTÉ MEDIUM**. Working in batches to avoid crowding the meat in the pot (which will cause it to steam instead of sear), cook the meat until well browned on all sides, turning with tongs, about 3 minutes per side. When sufficiently browned, the meat will release from

(recipe continues)

1 tablespoon packed dark
brown sugar

1 (12-ounce) bottle dark beer,
such as a Mexican lager

¼ cup masa harina
or fine cornmeal

2 tablespoons apple cider
vinegar, preferably unfiltered

———∞———

*Serve with: thinly sliced scallions,
diced avocado, lime wedges, and
warmed corn tortillas*

the pot without tugging or tearing. Don't rush this step. It's critical to the flavor of the dish. Transfer the browned meat to a bowl. Reduce the heat if the browned glaze on the bottom of the pot begins to scorch. Add more oil if needed between batches.

8. Add more oil to the pan, if needed, and cook the onion until softened and golden, about 8 minutes. Stir in the garlic, cumin, cinnamon, and brown sugar and cook until fragrant, about 30 seconds. Stir in the beer and bring to a simmer, stirring to loosen every speck of browned glaze and bits from the bottom of the pot. (The multicooker might issue a burn warning message if there are solids stuck to the bottom of the pot during pressure-cooking.)

9. Return the beef and any accumulated juices to the pot. Stir in the reserved chile paste and masa harina. If the meat mixture is not submerged, pour in enough of the reserved cooking liquid to cover.

10. Cover and cook on **HIGH PRESSURE** for 30 minutes. **QUICK RELEASE** the pressure. Stir in the cider vinegar.

11. Serve hot with the scallions, avocado, lime wedges, and tortillas.

Indoor Brunswick Stew

Brunswick stew is a flagship Southern community stew intended to serve a crowd, often as an accompaniment to barbecue, with some of the wood-smoked pork going into the pot. It is traditionally cooked over an open fire for hours, sometimes all night long. Classic Brunswick stew is amazing when made that way, but sometimes we need to come inside and make a shortcut stew, and that's when a multicooker comes in handy. Smoky barbecue sauce cannot replace or replicate the smoke flavor from a real fire, but it speaks to the spirit of the dish and adds a little piquancy.

2½ pounds bone-in, skin-on chicken thighs

2 cups chicken stock, homemade (page 64) or store-bought

1 tablespoon unsalted butter

Kosher salt

3 cups fresh or thawed baby lima beans or butter beans (12 ounces)

3 cups fresh or thawed corn kernels (12 ounces)

1 (28-ounce) can whole peeled tomatoes, chopped with their juices

1 medium yellow onion, chopped (about 2 cups)

½ cup ketchup

½ cup smoky barbecue sauce

¼ cup apple cider vinegar, preferably unfiltered

¼ cup Worcestershire sauce

1 teaspoon smoked paprika

Ground black pepper

1 pound smoked pulled-pork barbecue, preferably not sauced

HINT
Some classic recipes for Brunswick stew recipes say that it should be served so thick that a spoon can stand upright in the pot. Very thick stews do not cook well under pressure in a multicooker, so if your stew turns out thinner than you prefer at the end of step 3, simmer it uncovered on SAUTÉ MEDIUM for a few minutes until it thickens to your liking, stirring often.

1. Place the chicken in the pot and pour in the stock. Add the butter, and ½ teaspoon salt. Cover and cook on **HIGH PRESSURE** for 10 minutes. Let stand for **NATURAL RELEASE** for 10 minutes, then **QUICK RELEASE** the remaining pressure.

2. Remove the chicken pieces to a plate and when they are cool enough to handle, shred the meat into large bite-size pieces. Place in a medium bowl, cover, and refrigerate until needed. Discard the skin and bones.

3. Strain the stock and return it to the pot. Discard the solids. Stir in the butter beans, corn, tomatoes, onion, ketchup, barbecue sauce, vinegar, Worcestershire, paprika, and 1 teaspoon each salt and pepper. Cover and cook on **HIGH PRESSURE** for 8 minutes. Let stand for **NATURAL RELEASE** for 10 minutes, then **QUICK RELEASE** the remaining pressure. Stir in the pulled pork and let stand for 5 minutes, stirring occasionally. Taste and adjust the seasoning, if desired.

Weeknight
Suppers

& Sunday
Dinners

Chicken and Fluffy Dumplings

There are as many ways to make chicken dumplings across the South as there are ways to fry those birds. Local loyalties run deep and people have their favorites. Mine are these fluffy biscuit-like dumplings that float like clouds atop a simple stew of large pieces of tender chicken studded with bright orange carrots and flecks of herbs. This meal is so comforting that it feels restorative.

Rich homemade stock that actually tastes like chicken is the bedrock of this stew. Twice-cooking the stock with meat and then with only the carcass deepens its flavor and doesn't take long in a multicooker. You can purchase a whole chicken and cut it into pieces (or ask the butcher to do it) or purchase packaged chicken that is already cut into serving pieces.

You will need a tight-fitting lid to cover the pot and hold in the heat while making the dumplings, preferably a tempered glass lid that will let you keep an eye on things. The heavy lid that comes with the multicooker is not a good option because on some models, it causes the **SAUTÉ** function to cut off.

STOCK AND COOKED MEAT

3 to 3½ pounds meaty bone-in, skin-on chicken pieces (from a cut-up whole chicken or a mixture of breasts and thighs)

2 tablespoons unsalted butter

3 large fresh thyme sprigs

1 teaspoon kosher salt

1 tablespoon distilled white or apple cider vinegar

STEW

1 tablespoon unsalted butter

1 medium yellow onion, chopped (about 1½ cups)

2 celery stalks, thinly sliced (about ½ cup)

3 medium carrots, cut into thin rounds (about 1½ cups)

1 tablespoon fresh thyme leaves

2 teaspoons kosher salt

½ teaspoon ground black pepper

3 tablespoons chopped fresh flat-leaf parsley

DUMPLINGS

1¼ cups all-purpose flour

2 teaspoons baking powder

1 teaspoon kosher salt

½ teaspoon sugar

½ teaspoon ground black pepper

2 tablespoons unsalted butter, cut into small cubes and chilled

2 tablespoons vegetable shortening or leaf lard, chilled

½ cup half-and-half, or as needed

1. For the stock and cooked meat: Place the chicken in the pot; arrange the dark meat pieces on the bottom and the split breast halves on top. Arrange the breasts so that they are nested together, skin-side down. Add 4 cups water, the butter, thyme, and salt.

(recipe continues)

Cover and cook on **HIGH PRESSURE** for 8 minutes. Let stand for **NATURAL RELEASE** for 5 minutes, then **QUICK RELEASE** the remaining pressure.

2. Transfer the chicken pieces to a plate. As soon as they are cool enough to handle, pull the meat from the bones and shred it into bite-size pieces. Save the skin and bones for step 3. Place the meat in a medium bowl, cover, and refrigerate it until needed.

3. Return the bones and skin to the pot. Add the vinegar. Cover and cook on **HIGH PRESSURE** for 15 minutes. **QUICK RELEASE** the pressure. Strain the stock through a fine-mesh sieve into a large bowl and set aside until needed. Discard the solids. Rinse and dry the pot and return it to the multicooker.

4. **For the stew:** Heat the butter in the pot on **SAUTÉ MEDIUM**. Add the onion, celery, carrots, and thyme and stir to coat. Cook until tender, about 5 minutes, stirring often. Stir in the reserved stock and chicken meat and season with salt and pepper. Cover with a tight-fitting tempered glass lid and select the **KEEP WARM** setting.

5. **For the dumplings:** Whisk together the flour, baking powder, salt, sugar, and pepper in a medium bowl. Work the butter and shortening into the flour with your fingertips until the mixture is crumbly. Slowly stir in enough half-and-half to make a soft, sticky dough that barely holds its shape on a spoon.

6. Uncover the pot and bring the chicken stew to a gently bubbling low boil on **SAUTÉ LOW**. (If the stew isn't warm enough to bubble, the dumplings will turn out dense and soggy. If the stew boils vigorously, the liquid will reduce too much.) Use a 1-ounce scoop or two spoons to drop dumplings the size of Ping-Pong balls evenly over the surface of the stew.

7. Cover with a tight-fitting lid that can hold in the heat, preferably a tempered glass lid that lets you monitor the bubbling stew and see the dumplings while they cook. Simmer until the dumplings are firm and fluffy, 15 to 20 minutes. Uncover and let stand 5 minutes. Sprinkle with parsley and serve warm.

Retro Cheeseburger Casserole

This recipe took America by storm in the 1950s and '60s when easy, one-dish dinners became popular. This family-friendly casserole delivers the flavors we love in a cheeseburger. All you do is spoon the ground beef filling into a dish and pour a quick batter over the top. As the casserole cooks, the batter rises to the top and sets, making a bready crust. A quick trip under the broiler browns the cheese on top. Serve the casserole with your favorite cheeseburger toppings and condiments. Mine are shredded lettuce, sliced tomatoes, a drizzle of Thousand Island dressing, and a few dill pickles.

1 pound ground beef chuck
or ground dark-meat turkey

1 medium yellow onion,
chopped (about 1½ cups)

¾ teaspoon salt

½ cup ketchup

2 tablespoons yellow mustard

2 teaspoons
Montreal steak seasoning

½ cup all-purpose flour

1 teaspoon baking powder

2 tablespoons unsalted butter,
cut into cubes and chilled

1 cup whole milk

2 large eggs

1 cup shredded Cheddar cheese

Serve with: your favorite burger toppings and condiments

1. Cook the beef and onion in the pot on **SAUTÉ MEDIUM** until the beef is no longer pink, breaking up the meat with the spoon, about 5 minutes. Use a slotted spoon to transfer the meat mixture to a 1½-quart round baking dish. Stir in ½ teaspoon of the salt, the ketchup, mustard, and Montreal steak seasoning. Rinse and dry the pot and return it to the multicooker.

2. Whisk together the flour, baking powder, and the remaining ¼ teaspoon salt in a medium bowl. Add the cold butter and use your fingertips to work it in until the mixture is crumbly.

3. Whisk together the milk and eggs in a small bowl, pour it into the flour mixture, and whisk until well combined. The batter will be thin and a little lumpy. Pour slowly and evenly over the meat mixture. Sprinkle the Cheddar over the top. Cover the baking dish tightly with aluminum foil.

4. Pour 1½ cups water into the pot. Set the baking dish on a metal trivet with handles and lower them into the pot. Cover and cook on **HIGH PRESSURE** for 30 minutes. Let stand for **NATURAL RELEASE** for 5 minutes, then **QUICK RELEASE** the remaining pressure.

5. Remove the dish from the pot and uncover. Position an oven rack so that the baking dish will be about 5 inches from the heat source and heat the broiler. Broil the casserole until the cheese is browned and bubbling, 2 to 3 minutes. Let stand for 5 minutes before serving warm with the desired toppings.

Green Curry and Buttermilk Vegetable Medley

This recipe was inspired by the best mango lassi that I've ever tasted, which was made with buttermilk. I tried it in this curry, and the buttermilk worked deliciously well. Some people say you can replace buttermilk with milk and a splash of lemon juice or vinegar, but buttermilk's lightly fermented natural cultures contribute flavor and perform culinary feats that curdled milk can never match or replicate. If buttermilk is truly unavailable, use another cultured dairy product, such as kefir or plain yogurt thinned with milk.

3 tablespoons ghee or unsalted butter

3 large shallots (about 5 ounces), peeled, halved lengthwise, and thinly sliced

1 serrano chile, thinly sliced

2 tablespoons finely chopped fresh ginger

2 tablespoons tomato paste

2 to 3 teaspoons green curry paste, to taste

1 teaspoon kosher salt

¾ cup light-colored vegetable stock or chicken stock, homemade (pages 65 and 64) or store-bought

1 medium sweet potato (about 8 ounces), peeled and cut into 1½-inch pieces (about 2 cups)

2 small parsnips (about 8 ounces), peeled and cut into 1½-inch pieces (about 1½ cups)

2 medium red potatoes (about 8 ounces), scrubbed and cut into 1½-inch pieces (about 2 cups)

2 cups cauliflower florets (about 8 ounces)

1 cup fresh or thawed corn kernels (about 4 ounces)

1 cup fresh or thawed petite green peas (about 4 ounces)

1½ cups well-shaken buttermilk

2 tablespoons cornstarch

2 cups lightly packed baby spinach (about 2 ounces)

WHEN TO GO LOW

The **LOW PRESSURE** setting on a multicooker is ideal for turning delicate vegetables tender without them breaking apart or overcooking.

1. Warm the ghee in the pot on **SAUTÉ MEDIUM**. Stir in the shallots, serrano, ginger, tomato paste, curry paste, and salt. Cook until sizzling and fragrant, about 1 minute, stirring constantly. Stir in the stock and gently scrape to loosen any glaze from the bottom of the pot.

2. Add the sweet potato, parsnips, potatoes, and cauliflower. Cover and cook on **LOW PRESSURE** for 4 minutes. **QUICK RELEASE** the pressure. Stir in the frozen corn and peas. (The stew is hot enough to cook them.)

3. Whisk together the buttermilk and cornstarch in a measuring cup and add to the vegetables while stirring gently. Stir gently until slightly thickened, about 1 minute. Just before serving, stir in the spinach. Serve at once.

Braised Pork and Apples
in Cider-Gingersnap Gravy

This dish is a bit like old-fashioned sauerbraten, a traditional German recipe for a sweet-and-sour meat stew, pork shoulder in this case. Subtle sweetness and spice mingle in each bite, thanks to a spice rub on the pork and a few crushed gingersnap cookies in the gravy.

Like many braised meat dishes, this one is best when made a day ahead of serving and refrigerated overnight so the flavors can come into their own. The chill time also allows the fat from the pork shoulder to solidify on the surface so it can be easily removed and discarded. If time won't allow for the overnight rest, skim off as much fat as you can before finishing the gravy. This is delicious served over Mashed Sweet Potatoes with Browned Butter and Lemon (page 140).

1 tablespoon kosher salt

1 teaspoon ground black pepper

1 teaspoon mustard powder

1 teaspoon garlic powder

1 teaspoon ground ginger

½ teaspoon ground mace or nutmeg

½ teaspoon cayenne pepper

2½ to 3 pounds boneless pork shoulder

2 tablespoons vegetable oil, plus more if needed

2 tablespoons unsalted butter, plus more if needed

1½ cups hard apple cider (or 1 cup unsweetened apple cider and ½ cup white wine)

1 large yellow onion, thinly sliced (about 3 cups)

1 fennel bulb, thinly sliced (about 2 cups)

¼ cup finely crushed gingersnap cookies

2 tablespoons apple cider vinegar, preferably unfiltered

2 tablespoons whole-grain mustard

3 medium apples, cored and quartered (peeled only if the skins are tough or blemished)

1 tablespoon fresh thyme leaves

1. Stir together the salt, pepper, mustard powder, garlic powder, ginger, mace, and cayenne in a large bowl.

2. Cut the pork into 3-inch pieces, blot it dry with paper towels, add it to the bowl, and toss to coat in the spice mixture. Cover and refrigerate for at least 1 hour or up to overnight.

3. Warm the oil and butter in the pot on **SAUTÉ HIGH**. Working in batches to avoid crowding the meat in the pot (which will cause it to steam instead of sear), cook the meat until well browned

on all sides, turning with tongs, about 3 minutes per side. When sufficiently browned, the meat will release from the pot without tugging or tearing. Don't rush this step. It's critical to the flavor of the dish. Transfer the browned meat to a bowl. Reduce the heat if the browned glaze on the bottom of the pot begins to scorch. Add more butter and oil if needed between batches.

4. Pour in the cider and stir to loosen every speck of the browned bits and glaze from the bottom of the pot. (The multicooker might issue a burn warning message if there are solids stuck to the bottom of the pot during pressure-cooking.) Return the pork and any accumulated juices to the pot. Add the onion and fennel. Cover and cook on **HIGH PRESSURE** for 60 minutes. Let stand for **NATURAL RELEASE** of pressure.

5. For the best flavor, uncover and let cool slightly, then refrigerate overnight. Discard the fat that collects and congeals on the surface. Wipe away any condensation from the outside of the pot before returning it to the multicooker. Rewarm on **SAUTÉ MEDIUM**. (If there's no time for an overnight rest, spoon as much fat as possible off the surface of the cooking liquid.)

6. Once the pork is warmed through, stir in the gingersnaps, vinegar, and mustard. Taste and adjust the seasoning, if desired. Place the apples on top of the pork. Cover and cook on **LOW PRESSURE** for 2 minutes. **QUICK RELEASE** the pressure. Serve warm, sprinkled with thyme.

Cube Steaks *in Mushroom Gravy*

Cube steaks are thin, round pieces of top round or top sirloin beef that a butcher flattens and then texturizes with a scary-looking, multibladed machine. The name refers to cube steak's characteristic pattern of small, square slits and indentations made by that process. Cube steak is an unpretentious, economical cut of beef that occupies a tasty middle ground between a hamburger and steak. You won't believe how tender this meat is when cooked under pressure in the brown mushroom gravy. If you can't find cube steaks, use minute steaks instead.

½ cup instant flour (see page 93) or all-purpose flour

1½ teaspoons kosher salt, plus more to taste

1 teaspoon ground black pepper, plus more to taste

½ teaspoon paprika

8 cube steaks (3 to 4 ounces each)

2 tablespoons unsalted butter, plus more as needed

5 ounces exotic mushroom blend or cremini mushrooms, sliced

1 tablespoon vegetable oil, plus more as needed

1 medium yellow onion, finely chopped (about 1½ cups)

1½ cups beef consommé, beef stock, or chicken stock (page 64)

2 tablespoons heavy cream

2 teaspoons fresh thyme or finely chopped fresh flat-leaf parsley

1. Stir together the flour, salt, pepper, and paprika in a shallow bowl. Lightly and evenly coat the cube steaks in the flour mixture, pressing lightly to help it adhere. Set aside 3 tablespoons of the remaining flour mixture to use in the gravy.

2. Warm 1 tablespoon of the butter in the pot on **SAUTÉ MEDIUM**. Stir in the mushrooms and cook until browned, 3 to 5 minutes, stirring constantly so that they brown instead of turning soggy. Transfer to a plate, spread them in a single layer, and set aside uncovered until needed.

3. Warm the oil and the remaining 1 tablespoon butter in the pot on **SAUTÉ MEDIUM**. Working in batches to avoid crowding the meat in the pot, add the steaks and let them cook undisturbed until browned on both sides, about 3 minutes per side. Transfer the browned steaks to a clean plate. Reduce the heat if the browned glaze on the bottom of the pot begins to scorch, and add a little more butter and oil between batches, if needed. Repeat browning the remaining steaks.

4. Reduce the heat to **SAUTÉ LOW**. Add the onion and ¼ cup of the consommé and stir well to loosen every speck of the browned glaze and bits from the bottom of the pot. (The multicooker might issue the burn warning message if there are solids stuck to the bottom of the pot during pressure-cooking.)

5. Sprinkle the reserved flour over the onions and stir to coat. Cook for 2 minutes, stirring constantly. (It takes 2 minutes to cook away the raw flour taste.)

6. Stir in the remaining 1¼ cups consommé. Return the browned meat and any accumulated juices to the pot, tucking them down into the liquid. Cover and cook on **HIGH PRESSURE** for 4 minutes. Let stand for **NATURAL RELEASE** for 5 minutes, then **QUICK RELEASE** the remaining pressure.

7. Stir in the reserved mushrooms and cream. Taste and adjust the seasoning, if desired. Sprinkle with thyme, and serve hot.

INSTANT FLOUR

I like to use quick-mixing, instant flour when making pan sauces and gravy because it is a type of all-purpose flour that dissolves easily into liquids without lumping. This type of flour also makes a light coating for meat (such as cube steaks). Two common brands are Wondra and Shake & Blend. They come in 13.5-ounce cylindrical cardboard canisters in the flour section of most grocery stores. Use regular all-purpose flour when instant flour isn't available.

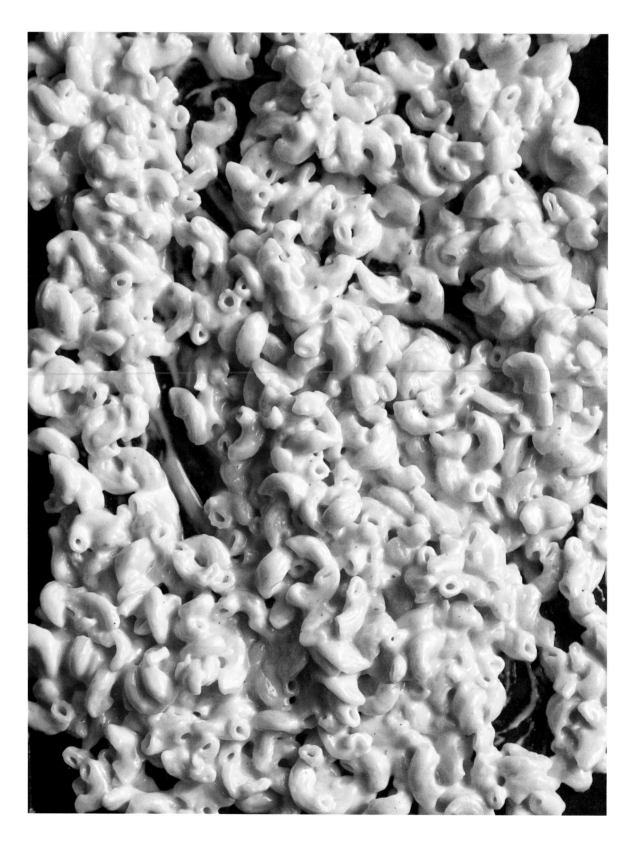

5-Minute Mac and Cheese

This is homemade comfort and joy, quicker and easier than ever because you do everything right in the multicooker. It's ready to serve in the time it would take to bring a pot of water to boil on a stovetop. This cheese sauce includes plenty of flavor from dried spices and a trio of cheeses, including Velveeta, which melts beautifully and makes the sauce smooth and creamy. If you like a little crunch on top of your mac, prepare the crumb topping from Summer Squash Casserole (page 137).

---

1 pound elbow macaroni

2 teaspoons mustard powder

½ teaspoon freshly grated nutmeg

⅛ teaspoon cayenne pepper

Kosher salt

3 tablespoons unsalted butter

1 (5-ounce) can evaporated milk, or ½ cup heavy cream

8 ounces sharp Cheddar cheese, grated

4 ounces Monterey Jack, Colby Jack, or Fontina cheese, grated

4 ounces Velveeta, diced

---

1. Stir together the macaroni, 4 cups water, the mustard powder, nutmeg, cayenne, 1½ teaspoons salt, and butter in the pot. Cover and cook on **HIGH PRESSURE** for 4 minutes. **QUICK RELEASE** the pressure.

2. Add the evaporated milk and half of the cheese to the pot. Stir until the cheese is melted. Add the remaining cheese and stir until melted. Taste and adjust the seasoning, if desired. Serve at once.

New Orleans–Style Barbecue Shrimp

Southerners are precise and querulous when it comes to barbecue. Although we cannot agree on how to prepare it, we are united in our insistence that barbecue is a noun, not a verb. Unless it's not. In this recipe, for example, the shrimp are not barbecued at all; they are braised in a pool of richly seasoned butter sauce that is reminiscent of barbecue sauce. Be sure to serve plenty of crusty bread to sop up every delicious drop.

New Orleans–style barbecue shrimp are usually cooked in their shells, but I tweaked the traditional recipe to use the power of pressure cooking to extract maximum flavor from the shrimp shells into the butter sauce, and then used gentle heat to cook the shrimp in that sauce. Please use the largest shrimp you can find for this recipe, because small shrimp won't turn out as tender and succulent as this great dish deserves.

2 pounds extra jumbo (16/20) shell-on shrimp

8 tablespoons unsalted butter

½ cup beer, preferably pale ale

8 garlic cloves, chopped

3 tablespoons Crystal hot sauce

3 tablespoons Worcestershire sauce

3 dried bay leaves

2 lemons, cut into thin slices

1 tablespoon chopped fresh rosemary, plus 1 teaspoon for garnish

1 teaspoon Creole seasoning

Serve with: lots of warm, crusty bread

1. Peel and devein the shrimp (reserve the shells for step 2) and place them in a medium bowl. Cover the bowl and refrigerate until needed.

2. Melt the butter in the pot on **SAUTÉ LOW**. Stir in the shrimp shells and cook until they turn bright pink, about 2 minutes. Stir in the beer, garlic, hot sauce, Worcestershire, bay leaves, lemons, rosemary, and Creole seasoning. Cover and cook on **LOW PRESSURE** for 3 minutes. Let stand for **NATURAL RELEASE** of the pressure.

3. Strain the sauce through a fine-mesh sieve set over a bowl, pressing firmly on the solids to extract as much liquid as possible. Discard the solids.

4. Rinse and dry the pot. Pour in the strained butter sauce. Bring to a simmer on **SAUTÉ MEDIUM**. Stir in the shrimp and cook only until they turn opaque, about 2 minutes, stirring constantly. The acidity of the butter mixture might ruffle the outside of the shrimp because they no longer have their shells to shield them, but they'll taste great.

5. Pour into a serving bowl, garnish with the rosemary, rush it to the table, and dig in with the warm bread.

Poached Salmon *with Creamy Herb Sauce*

Poaching might sound tedious, but it's easy and lightning-quick in a multicooker, which works like a steam oven. The salmon can be served warm, but it's the most refreshing on a hot summer day when served chilled. Be sure to use uniform center-cut salmon fillets that are about 1 inch thick so that they will cook evenly and optimally under pressure. Should you have leftover creamy herb sauce, it keeps well for up to a week and makes stellar salad dressing.

CREAMY HERB SAUCE

1½ cups crème fraîche (homemade, page 141, or store-bought), or ¾ cup plain Greek yogurt and ¾ cup sour cream

¼ cup fresh lemon juice (from about 2 lemons)

½ cup chopped fresh flat-leaf parsley

3 tablespoons chopped fresh dill

3 tablespoons chopped fresh basil leaves

3 tablespoons chopped fresh chives

3 garlic cloves, peeled and thinly sliced

1 tablespoon whole-grain Dijon mustard

2 teaspoons anchovy paste

⅓ cup extra-virgin olive oil

1 teaspoon kosher salt

½ teaspoon ground black pepper

SALMON

½ small yellow onion, thinly sliced (about ½ cup)

6 fresh parsley sprigs

6 fresh dill sprigs

8 skin-on center-cut salmon fillets (each about 4 ounces and 1 inch thick)

Kosher salt

16 thin lemon slices

1. **For the creamy herb sauce:** Place in a blender (in this order so that the herbs won't get tangled in the blades) the crème fraîche, lemon juice, parsley, dill, basil, chives, garlic, mustard, and anchovy paste. Blend until the herbs are very finely chopped. With the blender running, add the oil in a slow, steady stream. Season with the salt and pepper. Pour into an airtight container and refrigerate until chilled before serving, at least 30 minutes or up to 1 week.

2. **For the salmon:** Place 1 cup water, the onion, parsley, and dill in the pot. Lightly oil a metal trivet with handles. Arrange 4 of the salmon fillets skin-side down on the trivet. It's fine if the salmon hangs over the edges a little. Sprinkle the fillets with salt, top each with 2 lemon slices, and lower them into the pot.

3. Cover and cook on **HIGH PRESSURE** for 3 minutes. **QUICK RELEASE** the pressure. Transfer the cooked fillets to a plate. Cook the remaining 4 fillets the same way. Serve the salmon while still slightly warm or let it stand at room temperature until no longer steaming, then cover with plastic wrap and refrigerate until well chilled, at least 4 hours or up to overnight. Serve the salmon with the chilled sauce.

Slow-Cooker Pulled Chicken Sandwiches *in Cheerwine Barbecue Sauce*

MAKES 4 TO 6 SERVINGS

Sometimes I want the convenience and simplicity of boneless, skinless chicken breasts. To ensure the meat turns out juicy and tender, I cook it low and slow on the **SLOW COOKER** setting.

You can replace the zippy sauce with 2 cups of your favorite barbecue sauce. For the fiery flavor of Nashville-style hot chicken, add up to 2 teaspoons cayenne to the spice blend. I love to pile the pulled chicken onto toasted and buttered buns and serve it with pickles.

BARBECUE SAUCE

1½ cups Cheerwine or other cherry-flavored soda pop

1 cup ketchup

3 tablespoons Worcestershire sauce

2 tablespoons distilled white vinegar

1 large garlic clove, finely chopped

¼ teaspoon cayenne pepper

½ teaspoon ground black pepper

½ teaspoon mustard powder

2 tablespoons unsalted butter

PULLED CHICKEN

1 teaspoon kosher salt

1 teaspoon smoked paprika

½ teaspoon garlic powder

½ teaspoon ground black pepper

Pinch of cayenne pepper

2½ pounds boneless, skinless chicken breasts

1. **For the sauce:** Stir together the Cheerwine, ketchup, Worcestershire sauce, vinegar, garlic, cayenne, pepper, mustard, and butter in the pot. Bring to a simmer on **SAUTÉ MEDIUM**, stirring until the butter melts. Simmer, uncovered, until the sauce reduces to about 2 cups, about 30 minutes, stirring occasionally as the sauce thickens. Use immediately, or cool, cover, and refrigerate for up to 1 week.

2. **For the pulled chicken:** Stir together the salt, paprika, garlic powder, black pepper, and cayenne in a small bowl. Sprinkle over the chicken and toss to coat. Arrange the chicken in the pot and pour the barbecue sauce over the chicken. Cover and **SLOW COOK** on **LOW** for 5 hours. Remove the chicken to a bowl and cover to keep warm.

3. Simmer the sauce on **SAUTÉ MEDIUM** until it reduces enough to lightly coat a spoon, about 5 minutes, stirring occasionally.

4. Use two forks to shred the chicken into large bite-size pieces, return it to the pot, and stir to coat in the sauce. Divide the chicken among the buns, top with pickles, and serve warm.

Smothered Chicken

Smothered is an old-fashioned term for a dish that simmers in a sauce. In this recipe, browned chicken thighs and onion gravy cook together under pressure to the betterment of both: The chicken is tender and the gravy is full of flavor. For an old-fashioned, satisfying, comfort-food meal, serve the chicken and gravy over Long-Grain Dinner Rice (page 41) or Really Good Mashed Potatoes (page 136).

¼ cup instant flour (see page 93) or all-purpose flour

1 teaspoon kosher salt

½ teaspoon ground black pepper

1 teaspoon onion powder

1 teaspoon paprika

Pinch of cayenne pepper

6 bone-in chicken thighs, skin removed (about 2½ pounds)

1 tablespoon unsalted butter, plus more as needed

1 tablespoon vegetable oil, plus more as needed

2 medium yellow onions, halved and cut into thin strips (about 3 cups)

2 garlic cloves, finely chopped

1 cup chicken stock, homemade (page 64) or store-bought

2 tablespoons heavy cream (optional)

1 tablespoon fresh thyme leaves

1. Stir together the flour, salt, black pepper, onion powder, paprika, and cayenne in a shallow bowl. Lightly and evenly dredge the chicken in the flour mixture, tapping off the excess, and set aside in a single layer. Reserve the remaining flour mixture to use in the gravy.

2. Warm the butter and oil in the pot on **SAUTÉ MEDIUM**. Working in batches to avoid crowding the pot (and so the chicken can brown instead of steam), add the chicken and cook until deep golden brown on both sides, turning once with tongs, about 3 minutes per side. Add more oil and butter as needed. Transfer the browned pieces to a plate.

3. If the pot looks dry, add a little more butter and oil. Add the onions and garlic to the pot and stir well with a heatproof spatula to loosen the glaze and browned bits from the bottom of the pot. Add a splash of water if needed. Do not let the glaze scorch. Cook until the onions begin to wilt, about 3 minutes.

4. Sprinkle the reserved flour over the onions and garlic and stir to coat. Cook for 2 minutes, stirring constantly. (It takes 2 minutes to cook away the raw flour taste.) Add a splash of the stock if the mixture is too thick to stir and reduce the heat if the flour begins to scorch.

(recipe continues)

5. Add the stock and stir well to ensure that none of the flour mixture is stuck to the bottom of the pot. (The multicooker might issue the burn warning message if there are solids stuck to the bottom of the pot during pressure-cooking.)

6. Return the browned chicken thighs and any juices from the plate to the pot, nestling them into the gravy. Cover and cook on **LOW PRESSURE** for 8 minutes. Let stand for **NATURAL RELEASE** for 5 minutes, then **QUICK RELEASE** the remaining pressure.

7. Transfer the chicken to a serving platter.

8. Stir the cream (if using) into the gravy. Taste and adjust the seasoning, if desired. If you prefer thicker gravy, simmer it on **SAUTÉ MEDIUM** until it reduces to a consistency you are happy with. Pour the gravy over the chicken, sprinkle with thyme, and serve warm.

Bourbon and Cola Beef Short Ribs

This dish is inspired by the classic braised beef recipes that appear in almost all vintage community cookbooks in the South. The classic relied on a packet of dry onion soup mix for seasoning and a bottle of cola to help tenderize the beef. This recipe updates those flavors a bit. Instead of dry soup mix, the gravy includes fresh onions and herbs. Pressure-cooking ensures tender beef, but the cola is still here for flavor. Be sure to use cola sweetened with cane sugar that holds its flavor when cooked, such as one of the local, classic, or throwback soda pops that are popular and plentiful these days. I also add Southern bourbon. It all adds up to tender braised beef in exceptional gravy.

3 to 3½ pounds boneless beef short ribs

Kosher salt and ground black pepper

1 to 3 tablespoons vegetable oil, as needed

2 medium yellow onions, chopped (about 4 cups)

6 large garlic cloves, peeled and thinly sliced

1 cup cola, preferably sweetened with cane sugar (not diet)

3 tablespoons tomato-based chili sauce or ketchup

1 tablespoon Worcestershire sauce

1 tablespoon soy sauce

2 teaspoons dried thyme

1 teaspoon paprika

¼ cup bourbon

2 tablespoons fresh thyme leaves

1. Blot the meat dry with paper towels and then sprinkle it all over with 2 teaspoons salt and 1½ teaspoons pepper. Warm 1 tablespoon of the oil in the pot on **SAUTÉ HIGH**. Add the beef to the pot, working in batches to avoid crowding (so the meat sears and browns rather than steams). Let the short ribs cook undisturbed until deeply browned on all sides, flipping with tongs, 3 to 4 minutes per side. (When the meat is sufficiently seared, it will release from the pot without tugging and lift easily with tongs.) Transfer the browned pieces to a large bowl and repeat with the remaining pieces, adding more oil as needed if the pot looks dry. Reduce the heat and add a few drops of water if the browned glaze on the bottom of the pot begins to scorch or does not loosen. (The multicooker might issue a burn warning message if there are solids stuck to the bottom of the pot during pressure-cooking.)

2. Reduce the heat to **SAUTÉ MEDIUM** and add the onions and garlic. Stir to scrape up every speck of the browned bits and glaze from the bottom of the pot. Add a splash of water if necessary to loosen the browned bits. Cook until the onions begin to soften, about 3 minutes, stirring often.

(recipe continues)

HINT *Braised beef always tastes best the second or third day, so when time allows, let the finished dish cool to room temperature, which you can speed up by setting the inner pot in a large bowl or sink of ice water. When it's time to serve the dish, discard the fat that collects and solidifies on top. Wipe the outside of the inner pot dry, return it to the multi-cooker, and reheat the meat and gravy on WARM HIGH before serving.*

3. Stir in the cola, chili sauce, Worcestershire, soy sauce, dried thyme, and paprika. Cook for 1 minute, stirring constantly. Return the beef to the pot. Cover and cook on **HIGH PRESSURE** for 55 minutes. Let stand for **NATURAL RELEASE** of the pressure.

4. Use a spider or large slotted spoon to transfer the meat to a bowl, leaving the cooking liquid and vegetables in the pot. Spoon off as much fat as possible from the surface or use a fat separator.

5. Puree the cooking liquid and vegetables with an immersion blender directly in the pot. (Alternatively, purée in batches in a stand blender, filling it no more than one-third full with hot liquid. Return the puree to the pot.) Stir in the bourbon and season the gravy with salt and pepper.

6. Return the ribs to the pot, nestling them together and coating them in the gravy. Let the meat rest in the gravy on **WARM MEDIUM** until warmed through, about 20 minutes. Serve warm, sprinkled with fresh thyme.

VARIATION: Bourbon and Cola Brisket

Replace the short ribs with 3 to 3½ pounds first-cut brisket with its fat cap trimmed to ¼ inch thick. (If the brisket won't fit into the pot, cut it in half and sear it in batches.) After step 5, cut the brisket into ½-inch-thick slices (against the grain) and return them to the pot. In step 6, instead of just warming the brisket slices in the gravy (as you do with short ribs), cover and cook on **LOW PRESSURE** for 5 minutes. Let stand for **NATURAL RELEASE** of the pressure. Serve warm, sprinkled with fresh thyme.

Pickled Pepper Pull-Apart Beef

Versions of this wildly popular (and extremely simple) recipe have been passed around the South through conversation and social media posts. Pressure-cooking the chuck roast ensures that it turns out so tender that you don't even need to slice it. It just falls apart into large chunks, and it's ready in under an hour.

The pepperoncini make the cooking liquid piquant and delicious, so you'll want to serve this dish with something that can soak up some sauce, such as potatoes, rice, noodles, or crusty bread. Another great serving idea is to make hearty sandwiches: Pull the meat into bite-size pieces, moisten it with the cooking liquid, and tuck it into warm sub rolls. Top them with cheese slices and pile on more peppers.

2 tablespoons unsalted butter, cut into small pieces

4 pounds chuck roast

1 (1-ounce) envelope Italian or ranch dressing mix

1½ cups pepperoncini or banana pepper rings

½ cup brine from the jar of pepperoncini

1. Scatter the butter over the bottom of the pot. Add the roast. Sprinkle the dry Italian dressing mix over the top of the meat. Pour in 1 cup of the pepperoncini and the brine.

2. Cover and cook on **HIGH PRESSURE** for 50 minutes. Let stand for a **NATURAL RELEASE** of the pressure.

3. Uncover and let stand for 15 minutes, then spoon off the visible fat from the surface. Stir in the remaining ½ cup pepperoncini, or to taste. Serve warm.

Spring Vegetable Medley *with Fresh Herbs*

MAKES 4 TO 6 MAIN DISH SERVINGS OR 6 TO 8 SIDE DISH SERVINGS

Low-pressure cooking is the key to gently cooking these vegetables without them turning too soft and falling apart. The dish is a celebration of spring, hearty enough to serve as a main course, while being a lovely side dish as well. The liquid released by spring vegetables forms the heart and soul of the delicious sauce, so use tender, petite vegetables at the peak of freshness with skins so delicate that they don't even need to be peeled. You can mix and match produce to your liking, so long as you keep the total weight around 2½ pounds. Let the quality of the ingredients guide your selection. This is the perfect dish to prepare when you come home from the farmers' market with a little (or a lot) of everything.

8 fingerling potatoes (about 6 ounces), halved lengthwise (about 1½ cups)

8 baby carrots (about 6 ounces), halved lengthwise if larger than ¾ inch in diameter (about 1½ cups)

8 small turnips, such as Hakurei (about 4 ounces), halved (about 1½ cups)

8 small radishes (about 4 ounces), halved (about 1½ cups)

4 small golden beets (about 4 ounces), quartered (about 1½ cups)

1 cup Golden Vegetable Stock (page 65), light-colored vegetable stock, or water

3 tablespoons unsalted butter or extra-virgin olive oil

1 tablespoon sugar

1 teaspoon kosher salt

1 cup sugarsnap peas (about 4 ounces)

1 cup asparagus cut into 3-inch lengths (about 4 ounces)

1 cup fresh or thawed petite green peas or edamame (about 4 ounces)

1 cup thinly sliced spring bulb onions, shallots, or baby leeks (about 4 ounces)

Finely grated zest of 1 lemon

3 tablespoons finely chopped tender herbs, such as chervil, chives, and/or tarragon

HINT *Trimmed and packaged root vegetables cannot deliver the flavor of those with their greens still attached. Select bunches with greens that look good enough to eat, even when you don't intend to. Bright, perky greens with no wilting or blackening indicate fresh produce that hasn't begun to dry out and turn pithy.*

1. Combine the potatoes, carrots, turnips, radishes, beets, stock, butter, sugar, and salt in the pot. Cover and cook on **LOW PRESSURE** for 1 minute. **QUICK RELEASE** the pressure. The vegetables should be just tender enough to pierce with a knife. Don't let the vegetables turn mushy and break apart.

2. Stir in the sugar snaps, asparagus, peas, and onions. Cook on **SAUTÉ LOW** until the asparagus is just crisp-tender, about 2 minutes, stirring gently from time to time.

3. Stir in the lemon zest and fresh herbs. Taste and adjust the seasoning, if desired. Serve at once.

Country Captain

This gorgeous chicken dish is an old recipe that dates back to colonial times. It hails from the Lowcountry around Charleston and Savannah, an area known for great cross-cultural Southern cooking that makes brilliant use of the exotic spices that once arrived aboard ships that sailed into the deep harbors. If you've made Country Captain in the past, you'll be delighted by how much quicker it is to prepare in a multicooker. If you're new to the dish, you'll be thrilled to have another great chicken recipe in your repertoire.

3 ounces thick-cut smoky bacon (about 3 slices), diced

2½ pounds boneless, skinless chicken thighs

1 teaspoon kosher salt

¾ teaspoon ground black pepper

Vegetable oil

1 large yellow onion, halved and thinly sliced (about 2 cups)

2 medium red, yellow, and/or orange bell peppers, cut into ½-inch-wide strips (about 3 cups)

3 celery stalks with leaves, thinly sliced (about 1 cup)

4 garlic cloves, thinly sliced

1 tablespoon red curry powder (see page 66)

2 cups canned crushed tomatoes in puree

⅓ cup dried currants or golden raisins, plus extra for serving

Serve with: Long-Grain Dinner Rice (page 41) fruit chutney, flaked coconut, roasted peanuts or slivered almonds, and/or chopped scallions

1. Cook the bacon in the pot on **SAUTÉ MEDIUM** until crisp and rendered, about 8 minutes, stirring occasionally. Transfer the bacon to a small bowl and set aside. Leave the fat in the pot.

2. Season the chicken thighs with the salt and pepper. Working in batches to avoid crowding, add the chicken and cook until browned on all sides, about 2 minutes per side. Remove the browned chicken to a bowl. Add 1 tablespoon oil to the pan if needed between batches.

3. Stir in the onion and cook until it begins to wilt, about 2 minutes. Stir to completely loosen any glaze and browned bits from the bottom of the pot. Add a splash of water if needed to help loosen the glaze.

4. Stir in the bell peppers, celery, and garlic and cook until the garlic is fragrant, about 1 minute. Stir in the red curry powder and cook until it releases its aroma, about 1 minute, stirring constantly. Add the tomatoes and currants, and stir to make sure that none of the vegetable mixture has stuck to the bottom of the pot.

5. Return the chicken and juices to the pot, gently pushing them into the vegetable mixture. Cover and cook on **LOW PRESSURE** for 6 minutes. Let stand for **NATURAL RELEASE** for 5 minutes, then **QUICK RELEASE** the remaining pressure. Taste and adjust the seasoning, if desired. Serve over rice and with the reserved bacon and other condiments on the side.

Holiday Ham *with Ginger-Peach Glaze*

A multicooker makes a centerpiece ham so quick and easy that you can make one any old time. The glaze is the perfect finishing touch, broiled until bubbling and sticky. Peach preserves are delicious, but you can use pineapple, apricot, or even pepper jelly for a bit of sweet heat. Consider the capacity of your multicooker when selecting a ham. A ham that weighs about 5 pounds and is no more than 8 inches wide should fit inside the pot, but if it simply won't slide in, trim off a bit of the widest part.

1 (4- to 5-pound) fully cooked semi-boneless ham

1 cup peach preserves

¼ cup Creole mustard or whole-grain Dijon mustard

1 tablespoon mustard powder

2 teaspoons ground ginger

1 teaspoon coarsely ground black pepper

½ cup premium ginger beer or ginger ale (not diet)

2 tablespoons bourbon

Juice of 1 lemon

1. Use a sharp, heavy knife to score the top and sides of the ham in a diamond pattern. Make diagonal cuts that are about ¾-inch deep and spaced about 1½ inches apart.

2. Stir together ¾ cup of the preserves, the Creole mustard, mustard powder, ground ginger, and pepper. Spread half of the glaze over the top and sides of the ham. Set the rest of the glaze aside.

3. Pour the ginger beer into the pot. Lower the ham into the pot, cover, and cook on **LOW PRESSURE** for 15 minutes. Let stand for **NATURAL RELEASE** for 3 minutes, then **QUICK RELEASE** the remaining pressure.

4. Lift the trivet out of the pot and transfer the ham to a large oven-proof skillet or rimmed baking sheet. Leave the cooking liquid in the pot. Spread the remaining glaze over the ham.

5. Position an oven rack so that the top of the ham will be about 5 inches from the heat source and heat the broiler. Broil the ham until the glaze is bubbling and browned and the diamond pattern opens up and gets crispy on the edges, 6 to 8 minutes. Let stand for at least 15 minutes before serving.

6. Meanwhile, make the jus. Simmer the cooking liquid on **SAUTÉ MEDIUM** until it reduces by half. Stir in the remaining ¼ cup preserves, the bourbon, and lemon juice. Simmer until warmed through, about 3 minutes. Serve with the ham.

Slow-Cooked Pulled Pork

MAKES ABOUT 8 CUPS COOKED MEAT (ABOUT 4 POUNDS) PLUS COOKING LIQUID

I live in North Carolina, where we take pork barbecue very seriously. This slow-cooked pulled pork is *not* barbecue. It's tender, juicy, delicious, and versatile pulled pork prepared using the **SLOW COOKER** setting on a multicooker. Some cooks prepare pulled pork under pressure so that it cooks more quickly. I am not one of them. I believe that pulled pork tastes best when cooked low and slow. It isn't as quick, but once the pork is prepped and in the pot, you can ignore it for hours.

This recipe yields about 4 pounds of delicious meat that you can sauce (or not) and then pile onto buns, drape over nachos, roll into burritos, spoon over rice, stir into recipes, or simply eat straight up. There's likely enough for multiple meals. Pulled pork is many splendored.

2 tablespoons smoked salt or kosher salt

2 tablespoons packed dark brown sugar

2 tablespoons sweet paprika

1 tablespoon cracked black pepper

1 tablespoon chili powder

1 tablespoon smoked paprika

2 teaspoons mustard powder

2 teaspoons garlic powder

2 teaspoons onion powder

1 teaspoon cornstarch

½ teaspoon cayenne pepper

½ teaspoon celery seeds

6-pound bone-in or 5-pound boneless pork shoulder

2 medium yellow onions, sliced (about 4 cups)

1½ cups dark beer or chicken stock (homemade, page 64, or store-bought)

½ cup apple cider vinegar, preferably unfiltered

2 tablespoons Worcestershire sauce

1. Preheat the oven to 475°F. Line a rimmed baking sheet with aluminum foil and set a wire rack inside the pan.

2. Make the rub by stirring together the kosher salt, brown sugar, sweet paprika, black pepper, chili powder, smoked paprika, mustard powder, garlic powder, onion powder, cornstarch, cayenne, and celery seeds in a small bowl.

3. Pat the pork dry with paper towels. Use enough of the rub to lightly and evenly coat the meat and set the rest aside to use in step 4. Place the meat on the wire rack with the fat cap facing up and roast until the meat sizzles and with a bit of char on the edges, about 10 minutes. Remove from the oven.

4. Place the onions in the bottom of the pot and sprinkle in the reserved rub. Pour in the beer, vinegar, and Worcestershire.

5. Carefully move the meat to the pot with the fat-side up. (I stab a fork into each end and use them as handles.) Cover and **SLOW COOK** on LOW until the meat is soft enough to pull apart with a spoon or tongs, 14 to 16 hours.

6. Transfer the meat to a bowl and let stand until cool enough to handle. Discard the bone, gristle, and large clumps of fat. Pull the meat into large chunks or shred with a fork.

7. Strain the cooking liquid through a fine-mesh sieve into a medium bowl and discard the solids. Spoon off as much fat as possible from the surface or use a fat separator.

8. Toss the meat with enough defatted cooking liquid to moisten it. Serve the meat warm, or let cool, cover, and refrigerate (or freeze) to use in other recipes.

Vegetables & Sides

Applesauce *with Peppered Honey*

This intriguing applesauce includes enough spice to remind you of chutney, but you can still taste the apples. When you're not sure which type of apple to choose, select a mixture. Their combined flavors, textures, and attributes tend to outweigh any shortcomings of a single variety. Some apple varieties collapse into soft pulp when cooked, while others hold their shape, so a mixture of apples means that this applesauce turns out a little chunky. You can add a few pears or quince to the mix, if you like, just to change things up and be fancy.

2 to 2½ pounds apples, peeled, cored, and quartered

½ cup apple cider, preferably unfiltered

2 tablespoons unsalted butter

½ teaspoon ground ginger

½ teaspoon mustard powder

3 tablespoons honey, or to taste

2 tablespoons sherry vinegar or fresh lemon juice

Kosher salt and ground black pepper

1. Place the apples in the pot. Add the cider, butter, ginger, and mustard and stir to coat. Cover and cook on **LOW PRESSURE** for 3 minutes. Let stand for **NATURAL RELEASE** of the pressure.

2. Stir in the honey and vinegar. Season with salt and more pepper than you might think. The sauce should be a balanced combination of sweet, tangy, and savory.

3. Serve warm, at room temperature, or lightly chilled.

Boiled Peanuts *for Snacking*

The best boiled peanuts are made with green, freshly dug peanuts during the fall harvest season, but the next best choice is raw peanuts that are common in grocery stores and roadside markets year-round. Don't attempt to boil peanuts that have already been roasted in the shell.

1 pound green or raw peanuts
in the shell, washed

3 tablespoons kosher salt

1 tablespoon regular
or hot Old Bay seasoning
or Cajun seasoning

1. Place the peanuts in the pot and add water to cover by 1 inch. Place a plate or something similar over them to keep them submerged. Cover and cook on **HIGH PRESSURE** for 60 minutes for green peanuts and 90 minutes for raw peanuts. Let stand for **NATURAL RELEASE** of the pressure. The doneness of boiled peanuts is personal, from al dente to quite soft. If they are too firm for your liking, cover and cook on **HIGH PRESSURE** for another 15 to 30 minutes, then let stand for **NATURAL RELEASE** of the pressure.

2. Drain and serve warm, at room temperature, or lightly chilled.

1 cup shelled Boiled Peanuts
(above)

¼ cup well-stirred tahini
or smooth all-natural
peanut butter

2 tablespoons fresh lemon juice

1 garlic clove, chopped

½ teaspoon ground coriander
or cumin

Pinch of cayenne pepper

⅓ cup extra-virgin olive oil

Kosher salt (optional)

1 tablespoon sesame seeds
or benne seeds

VARIATION: Boiled Peanut Hummus   MAKES ABOUT 1¼ CUPS

If you're willing to give up a few of your boiled peanuts, they make excellent hummus. Pulse the peanuts, tahini, lemon juice, garlic, coriander, and cayenne in a food processor until finely chopped. With the processor running, add enough oil to form a thick, smooth paste. Add salt, if needed, and then stir in the sesame seeds. Serve at room temperature or chilled.

Broccoli Pasta Salad
with Poppy Seed Dressing

This recipe brings together the flavors and fond memories of several classic Southern recipes made popular at potlucks and tailgates: creamy broccoli salad, pasta salad, and sweet poppy seed dressing. It's still quite good even without the bacon if you want to keep it meatless. Pasta cooks in less than half the time in a multicooker and the hot water quickly blanches the broccoli, turning it crisp-tender and bright green.

4 ounces thick-cut smoky bacon (about 4 slices), diced

8 ounces farfalle pasta

3 cups fresh broccoli florets cut into bite-size pieces (8 ounces)

½ cup mayonnaise

¼ cup sugar

3 tablespoons sherry vinegar

1 teaspoon mustard powder

1 teaspoon poppy seeds

1 teaspoon kosher salt

½ teaspoon ground black pepper

1 cup seedless grapes, halved

¼ cup thinly sliced shallots

½ cup pecan pieces, toasted if you like

1. Cook the bacon in the pot on **SAUTÉ MEDIUM** until crisp and rendered, about 8 minutes, stirring often. Use a slotted spoon to transfer the bacon to paper towels to drain. Pour the fat into a small jar to save for another recipe. (For goodness' sake, don't waste it.)

2. Place the pasta in the pot and add water to cover, about 4 cups. Cover and cook on **HIGH PRESSURE** for 4 minutes. **QUICK RELEASE** the pressure.

3. Add the broccoli and let it blanch in the hot water until it turns bright green and crisp-tender, about 1 minute, stirring slowly and constantly. Drain both the pasta and broccoli in a sieve and transfer to a large bowl.

4. Whisk together the mayonnaise, sugar, vinegar, mustard powder, poppy seeds, salt, and pepper in a small bowl. Add to the warm pasta mixture and stir to coat. Let stand until cooled to room temperature, stirring occasionally.

5. Stir in the grapes. Cover and refrigerate until lightly chilled, about 1 hour or up to 1 day. Just before serving, stir in the reserved bacon, the shallots, and pecans. Taste and adjust the seasoning, if desired.

Corn on the Cob
with Cotija-Ancho Mayonnaise

Vegetables steamed in a multicooker are not submerged in water, so nothing dilutes their flavor. If anything, the pressure-cooking enhances the corn flavor, so the freshness and quality of the freshly shucked ears is paramount. The zesty chile and cheese mixture that goes onto the cooked corn is inspired by *elote*, the Mexican-style corn served on sticks by street vendors. However, the cooking method is a great way to prepare corn to use in other recipes or to serve with other seasonings, such as good old butter.

½ cup mayonnaise

1 cup grated Cotija cheese or finely crumbled feta cheese, plus more for serving

½ teaspoon ground ancho chiles or chili powder, plus more for serving

4 ears corn, husks and silks removed

Lime wedges, for serving

1. Stir together the mayonnaise, Cotija, and ancho in a small bowl until well blended. Set aside.

2. Pour 1 cup water into the pot. Place the corn in a steamer basket and lower them into the pot. Cover and cook on **HIGH PRESSURE** for 2 minutes. **QUICK RELEASE** the pressure. Remove the corn from the pot and blot it dry with paper towels.

3. Coat the corn with the mayonnaise mixture. Sprinkle with a little more cheese and a dusting of ancho powder. Serve at once with lime wedges.

SHUCKING CORN

Although it can be messy to shuck corn at home, it's best to purchase ears still in their husks and remove them just before cooking. The freshest corn will have tassels that are dry, pale, straw-colored, and silky instead of dark and wet. Wipe away any silks clinging to the corn with a damp paper towel before cooking.

Fresh Cottage Cheese

Homemade cottage cheese is less creamy and has smaller curds than most store-bought varieties, and its incomparable flavor is a real treat. Many Southerners serve cottage cheese as a side dish, either solo or as part of a fruit or vegetable plate, or with a salad alongside, as I do here. I remember my grandmother making cottage cheese—she would have been awestruck to see a multicooker turn out a perfect version with little more than the press of a button. This recipe requires a multicooker with a **YOGURT** setting.

COTTAGE CHEESE

1 gallon 2% milk

¾ cup distilled white vinegar

1 teaspoon kosher salt

½ cup half-and-half
or heavy cream

SALAD

¼ cup mayonnaise

2 tablespoons finely chopped
red onion

4 teaspoons apple cider vinegar

½ teaspoon sugar

1 English cucumber, peeled
and cut into ½-inch dice

2 large tomatoes, cut into
½-inch dice

Kosher salt and ground
black pepper

1. **For the cottage cheese:** Line a large, fine-mesh sieve with a double thickness of dampened cheesecloth and set aside.

2. Pour the milk into the pot. Cover, select the **YOGURT** function, and adjust to the **BOIL** setting. When the cooking time is complete (usually 45 to 60 minutes), turn off the pot. Let stand, covered, for 1 hour.

3. Add the vinegar in a slow, steady stream while stirring gently. Let stand 20 minutes. Strain the mixture through the prepared sieve. Gently rinse the cottage cheese curds under cold running water. Transfer it to a bowl and stir in the half-and-half and salt. Cover and refrigerate until chilled, at least 1 hour or for up to 4 days. Taste and adjust the salt, if desired.

4. **For the salad:** Whisk together the mayonnaise, onion, vinegar, and sugar in a large bowl. Add the cucumber and tomato and stir gently to coat. Season with salt and pepper to taste. Cover and refrigerate for at least 30 minutes and up to 1 hour. Just before serving, stir the salad gently. Taste and adjust the seasoning, if desired.

5. To serve, spoon the cottage cheese onto serving plates and top with the salad.

A Deviled Egg Plate of Deviled Eggs

MAKES 2 DOZEN

You know a dish is beloved when it warrants its own serving vessel. Many Southern households can lay claim to at least one deviled egg plate (with small egg-shaped divots to perfectly cradle each halved egg), perhaps a family heirloom. If you don't have one, you can get those slippery eggs to sit upright on a flat tray by shaving a thin slice off the rounded bottom of the halved eggs to make them sit level—but it's more fun to have a deviled egg plate. Use this recipe as a guideline for making deviled eggs the way that you like them. There are many ways and traditions, and families can be particular.

1 dozen large eggs

¼ cup very finely chopped scallions (white and tender green parts only)

2 tablespoons fresh lemon juice or pickle, olive, or caper brine

1 tablespoon yellow or Dijon mustard

1 teaspoon hot sauce

4 tablespoons unsalted butter, at room temperature

4 to 6 tablespoons mayonnaise

Kosher salt and ground black pepper

Paprika, for dusting (optional)

1. Have ready a large bowl of ice water. Pour 2 cups water into the pot. Arrange 7 of the eggs on an egg rack and lower it into the pot. Stack a second rack atop the first, and arrange the remaining 5 eggs on it. Cover and cook on **LOW PRESSURE** for 8 minutes. **QUICK RELEASE** the pressure.

2. Immediately transfer the eggs to the ice water and let stand until cool enough to handle. Peel the eggs and blot them dry.

3. Halve the eggs lengthwise and drop the yolks into a bowl. Arrange the whites on a serving platter.

4. Mash the yolks with a fork. (For silky smooth filling, pass the yolks through a fine-mesh sieve into the bowl, using a spatula to push them through the mesh.) Stir in the scallions, brine, mustard, and hot sauce. Work in the butter. Add enough mayonnaise to make a thick, creamy filling that will hold its shape in the eggs. Season with salt and pepper. Taste and adjust the seasoning, if desired. Be sure to season the filling boldly; the flavor dulls a little when chilled.

(recipe continues)

5. Spoon the filling into the whites, mounding it slightly on top. (Alternatively, use a pastry bag fitted with a large tip or a zip-top bag with one corner snipped open to pipe the filling into the whites.) Sprinkle with more salt and pepper, plus paprika if that's your thing.

6. Serve soon or cover and refrigerate until lightly chilled. Deviled eggs taste best when not served stone cold straight from the fridge, so let them sit out at room temperature for a few minutes before serving.

COOKING TIMES FOR EGGS IN THEIR SHELLS, FROM POACHED TO FIRM

I am impressed by the range of foods that I can prepare in a multicooker, but I'd even buy one if the only thing it did was cook eggs in their shells. (Never again must I try to corral trailing egg whites when trying to poach eggs in a saucepan of water. Never again will I be abashed by ragged whites on my deviled eggs.) No matter the preferred cooking time, the eggs cook evenly and peel easily, so long as they go immediately from the multicooker to a bowl of ice water.

A metal egg rack that sits inside the multicooker is a great investment because it holds the eggs upright and in place so that they don't collide as they cook. When stacked, a set of two egg racks can hold up to a dozen eggs at once. Without a rack, cook no more eggs at once than can fit in a single layer in a steamer basket. For best results, don't attempt to cook fewer than 3 eggs at once,

whether in a rack or a basket. The only time I've had eggs blow out when cooked with **LOW PRESSURE** is when there were hairline cracks in the shells that I didn't notice before putting them into the pot.

Before you begin prepare a bowl of ice water to hold the cooked eggs. Cook the eggs on **LOW PRESSURE** for the desired time and then **QUICK RELEASE** the pressure. Immediately transfer them to the ice water. Leave the eggs submerged until they are cool enough to handle and peel, but no longer than 2 minutes when you want to serve them warm.

I use the times listed below to prepare large organic chicken eggs from the grocery store or farmers' market. Be aware that there can be slight variations in time depending on the size and freshness of the eggs, so experiment until you find the time that's perfectly suited to your eggs and doneness preference.

- **3 minutes:** poached eggs with warm, liquid centers
- **4 to 5 minutes:** soft-cooked eggs with barely set centers
- **6 to 7 minutes:** medium eggs with firm, moist centers
- **8 minutes:** hard-cooked eggs with powdery centers

Corn Pudding

This corn pudding is so light and fluffy that it's more like soufflé than a casserole. When cutting fresh corn off the cob, be sure to scrape all of the milky liquid from the cobs with a spoon or the back of the knife. The corn milk adds flavor and the natural starch helps thicken the pudding. If using frozen corn, be sure the kernels are fully thawed and blot them dry.

Unsalted butter and all-purpose flour for the baking dish

4 cups fresh or thawed corn kernels

3 large eggs

¾ cup heavy cream

½ cup whole milk

¼ cup sugar

2 tablespoons unsalted butter, melted and slightly cooled

2 tablespoons all-purpose flour

2 teaspoons baking powder

1 teaspoon kosher salt

½ teaspoon ground black pepper

2 tablespoons finely chopped tender herbs, such as chervil, chives, parsley, and/or tarragon (optional)

1. Butter and flour a 1½-quart round baking dish.

2. Puree 2 cups of the corn, the eggs, cream, milk, sugar, melted butter, flour, baking powder, salt, and pepper in a blender. Pour into the prepared dish. Fold in the remaining corn kernels. Cover the dish tightly with aluminum foil.

3. Pour 1½ cups water into the pot. Set the covered dish on a metal trivet with handles and lower them into the pot. Cover and cook on **LOW PRESSURE** for 50 minutes. Let stand for **NATURAL RELEASE** of the pressure.

4. Remove the dish from the pot and uncover. Let stand for at least 15 minutes before serving barely warm, which is how this corn pudding tastes best. Garnish with herbs, if desired.

HINT *Compared to oven-baked corn pudding, this one will be pale on top when it emerges from the multicooker, despite being fully cooked. You can add color by garnishing the top with chopped fresh herbs or by placing the pudding under a hot broiler until the top turns golden brown in spots. Don't leave the dish under the broiler longer than necessary lest the pudding overcook.*

Family Reunion Potato Salad

I call this recipe Family Reunion Potato Salad because it's a slightly updated classic recipe that meets a range of potato salad expectations and suits most people, even across generations (even in my family). Like many potato salads, this one is best made a day ahead and it travels well, which makes it a great potluck contribution.

To keep the potato salad chunky, use small waxy yellow or red potatoes that hold their shape when cooked, such as Dutch Baby, Red Bliss, or fingerlings. Another secret to great potatoes in this recipe (beyond cooking them under pressure, which enhances their flavor instead of diluting it) is to season them with plenty of salt and something acidic (vinegar, in this case) while they are still hot so that they can absorb the seasoning as they cool. High pressure is usually too strong for hard-cooking eggs in their shells, but the potatoes shield them in the steamer basket, so they can cook together.

2½ pounds small waxy yellow and/or red potatoes, scrubbed

2 large eggs

¼ cup unseasoned rice vinegar or white wine vinegar

Kosher salt

½ cup mayonnaise

2 tablespoons yellow mustard

1 tablespoon Texas Pete or Crystal hot sauce

1 teaspoon celery seeds

1 small green bell pepper, diced (about 1 cup)

½ cup thinly sliced scallions (white and tender green parts only)

¼ cup diced pimientos, drained

¼ cup sweet-hot or dill pickle relish, drained

¼ cup coarsely chopped fresh flat-leaf parsley

Ground black pepper

1. Pour 1½ cups water into the pot. Have ready a bowl of ice water for the eggs.

2. Quarter any potatoes larger than a golf ball and halve the rest. Place the potatoes in a steam basket. Lower the basket into the pot. Rest the eggs atop the potatoes. Cover and cook on **HIGH PRESSURE** for 5 minutes. **QUICK RELEASE** the pressure. Transfer the eggs to the ice water to cool.

3. Transfer the potatoes to a large, shallow bowl and let them stand until they steam dry, about 3 minutes. Drizzle the vinegar over the potatoes and sprinkle them with 2 teaspoons salt. Let stand until cool, tossing occasionally.

4. Stir in the mayonnaise, mustard, hot sauce, and celery seeds.

5. Peel and chop the eggs. Fold the eggs, bell pepper, scallions, pimientos, pickle relish, and parsley into the potato mixture. Season generously with salt and pepper.

6. For best flavor, cover and refrigerate until deeply chilled, preferably overnight. Stir well and then taste and adjust the seasoning, if desired.

Quick Greens, *Three Ways*

I could barely contain my delight the first time I cooked leafy greens in a multicooker. After only 2 minutes, they emerged bright green, pliant, and just tender enough. Unlike greens sautéed in a skillet on the stovetop, they don't lose their volume and shrink away to nothing. This technique works best for leafy greens of medium sturdiness, such as kale, mustard, turnip, chard, mixed braising greens, very young collards, and the like. The leaves should be sturdy enough to not dissolve or turn slick when cooked (as spinach does), and yet tender enough for quick cooking to be sufficient.

Quick greens are plenty delicious served as a warm salad with nothing more than a drizzle of olive oil and a little salt and pepper, but when you want something a bit more elaborate as a finishing touch, turn to one of the recipes that follow.

12 ounces leafy greens, tough center ribs and stems discarded and leaves
cut into bite-size pieces
(about 10 lightly packed cups)

Extra-virgin olive oil

Kosher salt and ground black pepper

1. Pour 1½ cups water into the pot. Place the greens in a deep steamer basket and lower it into the pot.

2. Cover and cook on **LOW PRESSURE** for 2 minutes. **QUICK RELEASE** the pressure. Lift the basket out of the pot and shake gently to remove any clinging water.

3. If using the greens in one of the following recipes, set them aside until needed.

4. If serving them now, pour into a bowl and season with oil, salt, and pepper. Serve warm or at room temperature.

A HANDY STEAMER BASKET

A steamer basket is necessary for some multicooker recipes. They come in all sorts of shapes and sizes, but a tall mesh basket that nearly fills the pot is my pick. The basket's large capacity means it can hold the most food without any of it tumbling into the water, and a sturdy hinged handle makes it easiest to move in and out of the pot.

(recipe continues)

MEDITERRANEAN-STYLE QUICK GREENS

Quick Greens
(page 131), prepared
through step 2

¼ cup golden raisins

3 tablespoons sherry vinegar

¼ cup extra-virgin olive oil

4 garlic cloves, thinly sliced

¼ cup pine nuts

Big pinch of red pepper flakes

Kosher salt and ground
black pepper

The greens are enhanced by the sweetness of raisins, the crunch of pine nuts, and the acidic tang of good vinegar. Each element should be perceptible, and none should outshine the greens.

1. Set the greens aside in the steamer basket until needed. Empty and dry the pot.

2. Stir together the raisins and vinegar in a small bowl. Set aside so that the raisins plump in the vinegar. (To speed up the absorption, microwave for 30 seconds.)

3. Warm the oil in the pot on **SAUTÉ LOW**. Stir in the garlic, pine nuts, and pepper flakes and cook until the garlic and nuts are golden and sizzling, about 3 minutes, stirring often. Do not let the garlic burn.

4. Add the greens in large handfuls, tossing with tongs to coat. Mix in the raisins and vinegar. Season with salt and black pepper. Serve warm or pour onto a serving platter and let cool to room temperature.

SOUTHERN-STYLE QUICK GREENS

Quick Greens
(page 131), prepared
through step 2

4 ounces thick-cut smoky bacon
(about 4 slices), diced

½ small red onion, thinly sliced
(about ½ cup)

3 tablespoons apple cider
vinegar, preferably unfiltered

2 tablespoons packed light
brown sugar

Big pinch of red pepper flakes

Kosher salt and ground
black pepper

You can add a thinly sliced apple or finely chopped tomato to this recipe when you add the onion. The recipe is amiable and adaptable.

1. Set the greens aside in the steamer basket until needed. Empty and dry the pot.

2. Cook the bacon on **SAUTÉ MEDIUM** until crisp and rendered, about 8 minutes. Use a slotted spoon to transfer it to a bowl, leaving the fat in the pot.

3. Stir in the onion and cook until wilted, about 2 minutes, stirring often. Stir in the vinegar, brown sugar, and pepper flakes.

4. Add the greens in large handfuls, tossing with tongs to coat. Stir in the reserved bacon. Season with salt and black pepper. Serve warm or pour onto a serving platter and let cool to room temperature.

Height of Summer Ratatouille

Come July and August when garden-fresh vegetables pour in at a rate that can feel almost overwhelming, my solution is to make lots of ratatouille. It's a delicious side dish to grilled meat and seafood, but it is robust enough to serve as a meatless entrée, perhaps atop pasta or cheese grits (page 26), or with a hunk of crunchy garlic bread. It's also good served at room temperature. Crumble a little goat cheese or shave a little Parmesan on top, if you like.

1 pound very ripe tomatoes (see Hint, opposite), or 1 (28-ounce) can whole peeled tomatoes, chopped with their juices (about 4 cups)

2 teaspoons kosher salt

1 teaspoon ground black pepper

¼ cup extra-virgin olive oil, plus more for drizzling

1 medium yellow onion, chopped (about 2 cups)

6 garlic cloves, thinly sliced

1 teaspoon *herbes de Provence* or Italian seasoning

2 small zucchini (about 10 ounces), cut into 2-inch chunks (about 2 cups)

2 small yellow squash (about 10 ounces), cut into 2-inch chunks (about 2 cups)

1 small eggplant (about 10 ounces), cut into 2-inch chunks (about 2 cups)

2 medium red, orange, or yellow bell peppers, cut into 1-inch pieces (about 2 cups)

2 tablespoons sherry vinegar

1 tablespoon sugar

½ cup thinly sliced fresh basil leaves

> HINT *Peel the squash and zucchini only if the skins are so tough that you cannot nick them with a fingernail. Likewise, if they are so big that they are full of large, tough, gloppy seeds, scoop them out with a spoon and use only the firm flesh. All in all, smaller vegetables taste best and require less prep work.*

1. Stir together the tomatoes, salt, and black pepper in a medium bowl and let stand while preparing the other ingredients, stirring occasionally to encourage them to release their juices. When you are ready to cook the ratatouille, tilt the bowl to pond the juice in one corner. The multicooker needs at least ½ cup of liquid inside to come up to pressure, so if there is less than ½ cup of tomato juice, add water to make up the difference.

2. Warm the oil in the pot on **SAUTÉ MEDIUM**. Stir in the onion and cook until it begins to soften, about 3 minutes. Stir in the garlic and dried herbs and cook until fragrant, about 30 seconds, stirring often.

HINT *The tomatoes in this recipe must be flavorful and provide adequate liquid. If your fresh tomatoes are not juicy and brimming with flavor, use canned whole tomatoes instead. There needs to be at least ½ cup of liquid inside a multicooker for it to reach pressure, so whether fresh or canned, if your chopped tomatoes yield too little juice, add water to make up the difference. You can always reduce the cooking liquid at the end to ensure the dish doesn't turn out too soupy.*

3. Stir in the tomatoes and their liquid, the zucchini, squash, eggplant, and bell peppers. Cover and cook on **LOW PRESSURE** for 3 minutes. **QUICK RELEASE** the pressure. Use a spider or slotted spoon to transfer the vegetables to a serving bowl.

4. Simmer the cooking liquid on **SAUTÉ MEDIUM** until reduced to the consistency of sauce, about 5 minutes.

5. Stir in the vinegar and sugar, and stir into the vegetables. Taste and adjust the seasoning, if desired.

6. Serve warm or at room temperature. Just before serving, stir in the basil and drizzle with more olive oil.

Really Good Mashed Potatoes

MAKES 8 SERVINGS

Because potatoes steamed in a multicooker are never submerged in water, none of their pure flavor is diluted, making them notably potato-y potatoes. I remain convinced that russet potatoes make the best mashed potatoes, and I prefer small potatoes over huge baking potatoes because I think they have superior texture when mashed. You can use another potato if you like, so long as it is a starchy variety (such as Yukon Gold) that will collapse and turn fluffy when cooked. For perfectly smooth puree, pass the cooked potatoes through a food mill. Hand-mashed potatoes turn out a bit rustic, albeit tasty.

Kosher salt

3 pounds small russet potatoes, peeled and cut into 3-inch chunks

½ cup cream cheese, at room temperature (4 ounces)

½ cup sour cream or crème fraîche (homemade, page 141, or store-bought)

3 tablespoons unsalted butter, at room temperature

¼ cup whole milk or buttermilk, plus more as needed

1. Pour 1½ cups water and 1 tablespoon salt into the pot. Place the potatoes in a steamer basket and lower into the pot. Cover and cook on **HIGH PRESSURE** for 10 minutes. Let stand for **NATURAL RELEASE** for 10 minutes, then **QUICK RELEASE** the remaining pressure.

2. Lift the basket out of the pot and let stand until any water clinging to the potatoes steams away and their edges look chalky, about 3 minutes. Empty and dry the pot and return it to the multicooker set to **WARM MEDIUM.** Pass the hot potatoes through a food mill into the pot. (Alternatively, pour the potatoes into the pot, crush them with a hand-held masher, and then beat them as smooth as possible with a wooden spoon.) Do not mash potatoes with anything that has to be plugged in. It turns them gluey and you'll be sorry.

3. Add the cream cheese, sour cream, and butter to the warm potatoes and stir until melted and smooth. Stir in enough milk to make a thick puree.

4. Season generously with salt and serve warm.

> HINT *To make these potatoes up to 2 days ahead, leave them in the removable inner pot until cool, then cover and refrigerate. Wipe away any moisture on the inner pot before replacing in the machine, and reheat on WARM HIGH, stirring often. (Alternatively, transfer the potatoes to a buttered 2½-quart baking dish, cover, and refrigerate. Bake uncovered in a 350°F oven until hot and lightly browned on top, about 45 minutes. Or, reheat them in a microwave, stirring often.)*

Summer Squash Casserole

For the best flavor and texture, look beyond the common yellow crookneck and try Zephyr, cousa, and patty pan. Select small, young, and tender squash that don't need to be peeled and aren't loaded with large seeds.

CASSEROLE

Unsalted butter and all-purpose flour for the baking dish

1½ pounds mixed summer squashes, cut into ½-inch pieces (about 6 cups)

1 small yellow onion, finely chopped (about 1 cup)

2 garlic cloves, finely chopped

1 cup sour cream

2 large eggs, beaten

2 teaspoons chopped fresh thyme

1½ teaspoons Old Bay seasoning

½ teaspoon ground black pepper

1 cup soft fresh breadcrumbs

½ cup shredded Gruyère cheese (2 ounces)

CRUMB TOPPING

1 cup soft fresh breadcrumbs

½ cup shredded Gruyère cheese (2 ounces)

2 tablespoons unsalted butter, melted

1. **For the casserole:** Butter and flour a 1½-quart round baking dish. Pour 1½ cups water into the pot. Place the squash in a steamer basket and lower it into the pot. Cover and cook on **LOW PRESSURE STEAM** for 2 minutes. Let stand for **NATURAL RELEASE** for 5 minutes, then **QUICK RELEASE** the remaining pressure. Drain the squash well in a fine-mesh sieve, pressing to remove as much liquid as possible.

2. Transfer the squash to a medium bowl. Stir in the onion, garlic, sour cream, eggs, thyme, Old Bay, pepper, breadcrumbs, and Gruyère. Pour the mixture into the prepared baking dish and cover it tightly with aluminum foil.

3. Set the dish on a metal trivet with handles and lower them into the pot. Cover and cook on **LOW PRESSURE** for 12 minutes. Let stand for **NATURAL RELEASE** for 5 minutes, then **QUICK RELEASE** the remaining pressure. Remove the dish from the pot, uncover, and let stand while preparing the topping and heating the broiler.

4. **For the crumb topping:** Position an oven rack so that the baking dish will be about 5 inches from the heat source and heat the broiler. Toss together the breadcrumbs, Gruyère, and the melted butter in a small bowl. Sprinkle over the top of the casserole. Broil the casserole until the crumb topping is golden brown, 2 to 3 minutes. Let stand for 10 minutes and serve warm.

> HINT *You can toast the breadcrumbs in the pot while the casserole cools. After you remove the casserole, empty and dry the pot and return it to the multicooker. Warm the butter on* SAUTÉ LOW, *stir in the crumbs, and cook until golden, stirring often. Pour into a bowl, toss with the Gruyère, and sprinkle on the casserole.*

Summer Beans *in Fresh Tomato Sauce*

MAKES 4 TO 6 SERVINGS

This dish is stunning when made with a medley of yellow wax beans and emerald haricots verts bathed in golden tomato sauce, but feel free to use any type of fresh beans, including reliable everyday green beans. The key is to use tender, stringless beans that can be served whole with only their tips trimmed. Similarly, you can replace the yellow tomatoes with another variety, so long as the tomatoes are dripping with juice and flavor. The technique of creating a quick tomato sauce by rubbing halved, dead-ripe tomatoes on a box grater is a keeper, especially when you need to use up tomatoes that are too soft to slice, even the ones that burst on your way home from the farmers' market. The empty tomato skins wind up in your hand after all of the pulp passes through the grater, like magic.

3 medium very ripe tomatoes (about 1 pound), preferably yellow

Kosher salt

1 teaspoon sugar

3 tablespoons unsalted butter

1 medium yellow onion, very finely chopped (about 1½ cups)

2 garlic cloves, finely chopped

8 ounces fresh wax beans, ends trimmed

8 ounces fresh haricots verts or slender green beans, ends trimmed

2 tablespoons fresh lemon juice

1 tablespoon fresh thyme or lemon thyme leaves

Ground black pepper

1. Halve the tomatoes. Grate the cut-side of the tomatoes on the large holes of a box grater into a bowl. Discard the tomato skins. Stir 1 teaspoon salt and the sugar into the tomato pulp. Set aside until needed.

2. Warm 1 tablespoon of the butter in the pot on **SAUTÉ MEDIUM**. Stir in the onion and cook until beginning to soften, about 3 minutes. Stir in the garlic and cook until fragrant, about 1 minute.

3. Stir in the reserved tomato mixture and the beans. Cover and cook on **LOW PRESSURE** for 5 minutes. **QUICK RELEASE** the pressure.

4. Stir in the remaining 2 tablespoons butter, the lemon juice, thyme, and black pepper to taste. Simmer on **SAUTÉ MEDIUM** until the tomato mixture thickens enough to coat the beans, 2 to 3 minutes. Taste and adjust the seasoning, if desired. Serve warm or at room temperature.

THE STRING THEORY OF BEANS

There are two broad categories of beans: stringless (with strings tender enough to be eaten or no strings at all) and string beans (with ropey, inedible strings that must be pulled from the pods, such as Greasy Beans, Half-Runners, Pole beans, and Romano.) Because string beans are allowed to grow until they are full of mature beans, their pods are tougher and must be cooked long enough for both the pods and the beans inside to turn tender. To use true string beans in this recipe, remove the strings, break the pods into bite-size pieces, cover, and cook on HIGH PRESSURE for 5 minutes in step 3.

Mashed Sweet Potatoes
with Browned Butter and Lemon

MAKES 6 SERVINGS

Sweet potatoes are a top crop in the South, and there are more varieties than you might think, with flesh ranging from white to vermilion to deep purple, although orange tends to be the familiar favorite. For the best flavor and texture, choose small sweet potatoes that weigh no more than 8 ounces each. Large, football-shaped sweet potatoes tend to be watery and stringy.

6 small sweet potatoes
(each about 6 to 8 ounces)

4 tablespoons unsalted butter

½ teaspoon kosher salt,
or to taste

½ teaspoon ground ginger

½ teaspoon freshly
grated nutmeg

⅓ cup peach preserves

2 tablespoons dry sherry
or bourbon

Finely grated zest and juice
of 1 lemon (about ¼ cup)

1. Peel the sweet potatoes and cut them into 1-inch chunks.

2. Melt the butter in the pot on **SAUTÉ MEDIUM**. Cook until the butter is dark golden brown and smells nutty, about 4 minutes, stirring occasionally. Immediately add the sweet potatoes and stir to coat. Stir in ½ cup water, the salt, ginger, and nutmeg.

3. Cover and cook on **LOW PRESSURE** for 4 minutes. Let stand for **NATURAL RELEASE** for 4 minutes, then **QUICK RELEASE** the remaining pressure.

4. Stir the potatoes vigorously to mash them as smooth as possible. (For a silky smooth puree, use an immersion blender.) Stir in the preserves, sherry, lemon zest, and lemon juice. Taste and adjust the seasoning, if desired. Serve warm.

HOMEMADE SWEET POTATO PUREE

To use the puree in other recipes (such as pie or casseroles), cook only the potatoes, water, and salt, omitting the butter, ginger, and nutmeg. Pass the cooked potatoes through a food mill or mash by hand. The puree must have the consistency of canned pumpkin. If necessary, drain the puree in a fine-mesh sieve set over a bowl, and refrigerate until thick, at least 3 hours and up to overnight. Store in an airtight container in the refrigerator for up to 3 days or frozen for up to 3 months.

HINT *Though browning butter is easy, it can quickly turn from perfect to burned in seconds. If you see black flecks floating in the butter, accept that it burned and begin again.*

Homemade Crème Fraîche

1. Crème fraîche is what Southern cooks once called clabber or clabbered cream. In the days before ubiquitous refrigeration, resourceful cooks had to figure out how to make the most of fresh cream that had to sit at room temperature for a while. During this time, natural good-for-us cultures in the milk began to grow and ferment, causing the milk to thicken and develop a subtle tang. (Crème fraîche tastes like a dreamy mixture of heavy cream and sour cream.) Traditional instructions for making homemade crème fraîche call for letting it sit on the countertop until it thickens, which can take from a few hours to a couple of days depending on the temperature of the room. The moist, steady heat of the YOGURT setting on a multicooker eliminates the guesswork.

   The beauty of crème fraîche—beyond its flavor and consistency—is that it doesn't separate when added to warm foods, such as soups and sauces: See Winter Squash Soup with Apple Butter Cream (page 72), Velvety Potato and Leek Soup (page 68), or Succotash with Herbed Cream Sauce (page 143). Crème fraîche can also be used in desserts, such as Quick Lemon Cream with Fresh Berries (page 166).

1½ cups heavy cream

½ cup plain yogurt with live, active cultures (see Hint)

HINT *The key to homemade crème fraîche is to use another cultured dairy product as the starter, such as plain yogurt, skyr, cultured sour cream, or kefir. Read the label to make sure the ingredient list specifies live, active cultures. After you make your first batch, you can use some of your homemade crème fraîche as the starter in subsequent batches. When stored in a jar with a tight-fitting lid, crème fraîche keeps in the refrigerator for up to 8 weeks.*

1. Stir together the cream and yogurt in a small glass bowl or jar that will fit inside the multicooker. Place the bowl in the multicooker, cover, select the YOGURT function, and adjust the time to 6 hours. (There is no need to use a trivet or add water to the pot, since this process does not require pressure.) At the completion of the YOGURT cycle, the multicooker will go into KEEP WARM mode. The crème fraîche can stay in the multicooker on KEEP WARM for up to 12 hours.

2. Cover and refrigerate until chilled, at least 2 hours. Crème fraîche keeps in the refrigerator for up to 8 weeks.

Succotash *with Herbed Cream Sauce*

MAKES 4 TO 6 MAIN DISH SERVINGS OR 6 TO 8 SIDE DISH SERVING; 6 TO 8 SERVINGS

Succotash is sublime when made with fresh beans and peak-of-season sweet corn, although this recipe still holds its own when made with frozen vegetables. A little bubbling cream sauce lightly coats the vegetables, made with fresh herbs and a big spoonful of naturally thick crème fraîche instead of flour or cornstarch. This side dish is hearty enough to serve as an entrée, especially when spooned over hot cornbread or biscuits. To make this dish meatless, omit the bacon and replace the bacon fat with 2 tablespoons salted butter.

Butter beans are the term that some Southerners (including me) use to describe pale green or speckled brown lima beans that are eaten while still small and tender, which is why the frozen versions found in grocery stores are often called baby lima beans. When cutting fresh corn off the cobs, be sure to scrape every drop of sweet corn milk from the cobs, because the starch helps thicken the sauce.

2 ounces thick-cut smoky bacon (about 2 slices), diced

2 cups fresh or thawed butter beans or baby lima beans

1 teaspoon kosher salt

½ teaspoon ground black pepper

2 fresh thyme sprigs

2 cups fresh or thawed corn kernels

1 small red onion, finely diced (about 1 cup)

½ cup crème fraîche, homemade (page 141) or store-bought

2 tablespoons tomato paste

¼ cup lightly packed fresh basil leaves, thinly sliced

1 tablespoon fresh thyme leaves

1. Cook the bacon in the pot on **SAUTÉ MEDIUM** until crisp and rendered, about 8 minutes. Use a slotted spoon to transfer the bacon to a bowl, leaving the fat in the pot.

2. Stir in the butter beans and ¾ cup water, stirring to loosen every speck of the browned glaze from the bottom of the pot. (Multicookers might issue the burn warning message if there are solids stuck to the bottom of the pot during pressure-cooking.) Stir in the salt, pepper, and thyme sprigs. Cover and cook on **LOW PRESSURE** for 3 minutes. **QUICK RELEASE** the pressure.

3. Stir in the corn, onion, ¼ cup of the crème fraîche, and the tomato paste. Cover and cook on **LOW PRESSURE** for 3 minutes. Let stand for **NATURAL RELEASE** for 2 minutes, then **QUICK RELEASE** the remaining pressure.

4. Discard the thyme stems. Stir in the basil, thyme leaves, the reserved bacon, and the remaining ¼ cup crème fraîche. Taste and adjust the seasoning, if desired. Serve warm.

A Little Something Sweet

Chocolate Cream Pie

Cooking the chocolate pastry cream filling in a multicooker eliminates much of the stirring, although you will still need to strain the mixture to remove any small lumps, just as you would when preparing it on the stovetop. I always add cocoa powder to the whipped cream topping to double down on the chocolate.

FILLING

4 large egg yolks

½ cup granulated sugar

¼ cup cornstarch

¼ teaspoon kosher salt

2 cups whole milk

6 ounces semisweet chocolate, chopped, melted, and slightly cooled

2 tablespoons unsalted butter, chilled

1 teaspoon vanilla extract

1 (9-inch) baked and cooled pie shell

TOPPING

1 cup heavy cream, chilled

¼ cup powdered sugar

2 tablespoons unsweetened cocoa powder (not Dutch process)

1 teaspoon vanilla extract

Shaved or grated chocolate, for garnish (optional)

1. **For the filling:** Whisk together the egg yolks, granulated sugar, cornstarch, and salt in a medium bowl until smooth.

2. Warm the milk in a small saucepan or microwave until it begins to steam. Add the milk to the egg mixture in a slow, steady stream, whisking constantly until smooth. Whisk in the still-warm melted chocolate. Pour into a 1½-quart round baking dish. Cover the dish tightly with aluminum foil.

3. Pour 1½ cups water into the pot. Set the baking dish on a metal trivet with handles and lower them into the pot. Cover and cook on **LOW PRESSURE** for 18 minutes. Let stand for **NATURAL RELEASE** for 5 minutes, then **QUICK RELEASE** the remaining pressure.

4. Remove the dish from the pot and uncover. Use a heatproof spatula to loosen the pastry cream from the bottom and corners of the bowl, and then whisk as smooth as possible. Add the butter and vanilla and whisk until the butter melts.

5. Pass the warm pastry cream through a fine-mesh sieve set over a bowl, using the spatula to press it through. Pour the filling into the pie shell. Press a piece of parchment or plastic wrap directly on the surface to prevent a skin from forming. Let cool to room temperature, then refrigerate until chilled, at least 2 hours or up to overnight.

(recipe continues)

6. **For the topping:** In a stand mixer fitted with the whisk attachment (or in a large bowl if using a hand mixer), beat the cream, powdered sugar, cocoa, and vanilla on high speed to firm peaks. Spread over the pie and garnish with the shaved chocolate, if using. Chill the pie until ready to serve.

Coconut Cream Pie

Coconut has always been a favorite in Southern dessert recipes and this classic pie delivers a double dose: both inside (stirred into the pastry cream that's made in the multicooker and spooned into a pie shell) and on top. Just before serving, crown this glorious pie with swirled whipped cream and plenty of golden-brown toasted coconut, which adds crunch, flavor, and good looks.

FILLING

4 large egg yolks

½ cup granulated sugar

3 tablespoons cornstarch

2 cups whole milk

2 tablespoons unsalted butter, chilled

1 teaspoon vanilla extract

¼ teaspoon coconut extract

1½ cups sweetened flaked coconut

1 (9-inch) baked and cooled pie shell

1. **For the filling:** Whisk together the egg yolks, granulated sugar, and cornstarch in a medium bowl until smooth.

2. Warm the milk in a small saucepan or microwave until it begins to steam. Add the milk to the egg mixture in a slow, steady stream, whisking constantly until smooth.

3. Pour into a 1½-quart round baking dish. Cover the dish tightly with aluminum foil.

4. Pour 1½ cups water into the pot. Set the dish on a metal trivet with handles and lower them into the pot. Cover and cook on **LOW PRESSURE** for 18 minutes. Let stand for **NATURAL RELEASE** for 5 minutes, then **QUICK RELEASE** any remaining pressure.

5. Remove the dish from the pot and uncover. Use a heatproof spatula to loosen the pastry cream from the bottom and corners of the bowl where it will have thickened most, then whisk as smooth as possible. Add the butter, vanilla, and coconut extract and whisk until the butter melts.

6. Pass the warm pastry cream through a fine-mesh sieve set over a bowl, using the spatula to press it through. Stir in the flaked coconut. Pour the filling into the pie shell. Press a piece of parchment or plastic wrap directly on the surface to prevent a skin from forming. Let cool to room temperature, then refrigerate until chilled, at least 2 hours or up to overnight.

—∞—

1 cup sweetened flaked coconut

1 cup heavy cream, chilled

¼ cup powdered sugar

1 teaspoon vanilla extract

—∞—

7. **For the topping:** Preheat the oven to 350°F.

8. Place the coconut on a rimmed baking sheet and toast, shaking the pan once or twice, until the coconut is fragrant and golden brown, about 8 minutes. Pour the coconut onto a plate and set aside to cool.

9. In a stand mixer fitted with the whisk attachment (or in a large bowl if using a hand mixer), beat the cream, powdered sugar, and vanilla on high speed to firm peaks. Spread over the pie and sprinkle with the toasted coconut. Chill the pie until ready to serve.

Pecan Praline Cheesecake
with Shortbread Cookie Crust

Much of the success of a good cheesecake depends on timing, temperature, and accuracy. Thank goodness a multicooker can take care of that. The steamy air inside a multicooker is like a spa treatment for cheese-cake filling, turning it smooth, thick, and creamy with little risk of it splitting or cracking.

This cheesecake showcases pralines, those tender pecan-studded candies that are associated with New Orleans and taste like the best possible use of butter and brown sugar. Candied pecans, which are pecan halves with a light candy coating, are another Southern favorite. The confusion is that candied pecans are sometimes called praline pecans. The good news is that either praline candy or praline pecans will work in this recipe.

Pecans also appear in the cheesecake crust, which is made from finely crushed pecan shortbread cookies (such as pecan sandies), although you can use plain all-butter shortbread cookies or graham crackers, if you prefer.

CRUST

1 cup finely crushed pecan shortbread cookies (5 ounces)

1 tablespoon packed dark brown sugar

4 tablespoons unsalted butter, melted

1. **For the crust:** Position a rack in the center of the oven and pre-heat the oven to 350°F. Line the bottom of a 7-inch round spring-form pan with a round of parchment paper.

2. Toss together the cookie crumbs, brown sugar, and melted butter in a small bowl until the mixture resembles wet sand. Press firmly across the bottom and halfway up the sides of the prepared pan. Refrigerate for at least 15 minutes to firm up the butter.

3. Bake until just set, golden, and fragrant, about 10 minutes. Place the pan on a wire rack to cool to room temperature.

4. **For the filling:** In a stand mixer fitted with the paddle attachment (or in a large bowl if using a hand mixer), beat the cream cheese, granulated sugar, and brown sugar on high speed until smooth.

5. Add the sour cream, flour, and salt and beat on high speed until smooth.

2 cups cream cheese, at room
temperature (16 ounces)

¼ cup granulated sugar

¼ cup packed dark brown sugar

½ cup sour cream

1 tablespoon all-purpose flour

¼ teaspoon kosher salt

2 large eggs

1 large egg yolk

1 tablespoon bourbon

1 teaspoon vanilla extract

½ cup chopped candied praline
pecans or praline candies

TOPPING

½ cup sour cream

1 tablespoon packed dark
brown sugar

Candied praline pecan halves
or chopped praline candies,
for garnish

6. Add the eggs and egg yolk, one at a time, beating well and scraping down the bowl after each addition. Quickly beat in the bourbon and vanilla.

7. Sprinkle the chopped pralines over the crust. Pour in the filling. Cover the pan tightly with aluminum foil.

8. Pour 1½ cups water into the pot. Set the pan on a metal trivet with handles and lower them into the pot. Cover and cook on **HIGH PRESSURE** for 30 minutes. Let stand for **NATURAL RELEASE** for 8 minutes, then **QUICK RELEASE** the remaining pressure.

9. Remove the pan from the pot, uncover, and gently blot away the surface moisture with a paper towel. To minimize the chance of a cracked filling, run a knife blade around the inside of the pan so that the cheesecake won't adhere to the pan as it cools. Let it stand on the trivet until cooled to room temperature.

10. **For the topping:** Stir together the sour cream and brown sugar in a small bowl. Spread over the top of the cooled cheesecake. Refrigerate until deeply chilled, at least 4 hours, and preferably overnight. Run a thin knife around the inside of the pan to loosen the cheesecake and remove the pan ring. Just before serving, arrange the candied praline pecans on top.

Pineapple Upside-Down Cake

This classic cake with its sticky, buttery topping of brown sugar, pineapple rings, and cherries has been around for nearly a century, and we now have a new way to cook it. Cakes steamed inside a multicooker do not develop the browned crust they would in an oven, but the cake will be tender and springy. I like to add a little spice to the cake batter for good measure.

TOPPING

4 tablespoons unsalted butter, melted

½ cup packed light brown sugar

4 canned pineapple rings, drained (juice reserved)

4 or more maraschino cherries, drained

CAKE

1½ cups all-purpose flour

2 teaspoons baking powder

¼ teaspoon kosher salt

½ teaspoon ground cardamom

½ teaspoon ground cinnamon

4 tablespoons unsalted butter, at room temperature

⅔ cup granulated sugar

2 large eggs, at room temperature

½ cup whole milk

2 tablespoons dark rum, bourbon, or reserved pineapple juice

1 teaspoon vanilla extract

1. **For the topping:** Pour the melted butter into a 7-inch round baking pan. Sprinkle the brown sugar over the butter, stir gently to moisten, and then spread in an even layer. Arrange the pineapple rings and cherries in the pan, as desired, pushing them gently into the brown sugar mixture. Set aside until needed.

2. **For the cake:** Whisk together the flour, baking powder, salt, cardamom, and cinnamon in a small bowl.

3. In a stand mixer fitted with the paddle attachment (or in a large bowl if using a hand mixer), beat the butter and granulated sugar on high speed until light and fluffy, about 5 minutes. Add the eggs one at a time, beating well after each addition. Add the flour mixture in thirds, alternating with half of the milk, beating only until smooth after each addition. Quickly beat in the rum and vanilla.

4. Pour the batter into the pan, taking care to not dislodge the fruit. Cover the pan tightly with aluminum foil. Pour 1½ cups water into the pot. Set the pan on a metal trivet with handles and lower them into the pot. Cover and cook on **HIGH PRESSURE** for 50 minutes. Let stand for **NATURAL RELEASE** for 10 minutes, then **QUICK RELEASE** the remaining pressure.

5. Remove the cake from the pot, uncover and let stand for 10 minutes. Place a large serving plate over the pan and invert the cake onto the plate. Gently pry off any fruit that might have stuck to the pan and replace it on top of the cake. Let cool to room temperature before cutting and serving.

Red Velvet Cheesecake

Dessert lovers can't get enough of any sweet treat that sports the signature bright color of red velvet, including a great cheesecake. Red velvet desserts contain only a whisper of cocoa, but this cheesecake's crisp chocolate wafer crust ups its chocolate quotient. The moist environment and steady cooking temperature inside a multicooker is ideal for the creamy cheesecake filling.

CRUST

1 cup finely crushed chocolate wafer cookies (5 ounces)

1 tablespoon sugar

4 tablespoons unsalted butter, melted

FILLING

2 cups cream cheese, at room temperature (16 ounces)

½ cup sugar

½ cup sour cream

1 tablespoon all-purpose flour

1 tablespoon unsweetened cocoa powder

¼ teaspoon kosher salt

2 large eggs

1 large egg yolk

1 teaspoon vanilla extract

2 to 4 teaspoons red food coloring

1. **For the crust:** Position a rack in the center of the oven and preheat the oven to 350°F. Line the bottom of a 7-inch round springform pan with a round of parchment paper.

2. Toss together the cookie crumbs, sugar, and melted butter in a small bowl until the mixture resembles wet sand. Press firmly across the bottom and halfway up the sides of the prepared pan. Refrigerate for at least 15 minutes to firm up the butter.

3. Bake until just set and fragrant, about 10 minutes. Place the pan on a wire rack to cool to room temperature.

4. **For the filling:** In a stand mixer fitted with the paddle attachment (or in a large bowl if using a hand mixer), beat the cream cheese and sugar on high speed until smooth. Beat in the sour cream, flour, cocoa, and salt until smooth.

5. Add the eggs and egg yolk, one at a time, beating well and scraping down the bowl between additions. Quickly beat in the vanilla. Stir in the red food coloring until evenly mixed, ½ teaspoon at a time, until the color is as bold as you like. More coloring will make the cake a brighter shade, but some people do not care for the slight bitterness it imparts.

6. Pour the filling into the crust. Cover the pan tightly with aluminum foil. Pour 1½ cups water into the pot. Set the pan on a metal trivet with handles and lower them into the pot. Cover and cook on **HIGH PRESSURE** for 30 minutes. Let stand for **NATURAL RELEASE** for 8 minutes, then **QUICK RELEASE** the remaining pressure.

7. Remove the pan from the pot, uncover, and gently blot away the surface moisture with a paper towel. To minimize the chance of a cracked filling, run a knife blade around the inside of the pan so that the cheesecake won't adhere to the pan as it cools. Let stand on the trivet until cooled to room temperature.

8. Refrigerate until deeply chilled, at least 4 hours, and preferably overnight. Run a thin knife around the inside of the pan to loosen the cheesecake and remove the pan ring before serving. (Don't fret if there are a few small holes on top of the filling; that's normal for cheesecakes that steam in a multicooker.)

Sweet-and-Salty Key Lime Pie

The quirkiness in this pie comes in the crust, which is made with crushed crackers instead of cookies. Their hint of saltiness pairs well with the tangy lime filling and is echoed in the sweet and salty whipped cream topping. Citrusy condensed milk pies with cracker crusts are common in coastal North Carolina and are often made with lemon juice. In fact, you can replace the lime juice in the filling with lemon juice, as an easy variation.

CRUST

1 cup finely crushed round buttery crackers (such as Ritz) or saltines

2 tablespoons granulated sugar

4 tablespoons unsalted butter, melted

FILLING

1 (14-ounce) can sweetened condensed milk

4 large egg yolks

½ cup bottled key lime juice

SALTED WHIPPED CREAM TOPPING

1 cup heavy cream, chilled

2 tablespoons powdered sugar

1 teaspoon vanilla extract

Coarse or flaked sea salt, for sprinkling

1. **For the crust:** Position a rack in the center of the oven and preheat the oven to 350°F. Line the bottom of a 7-inch round springform pan with a round of parchment paper.

2. Toss together the crumbs, granulated sugar, and melted butter in a medium bowl until the mixture resembles wet sand. Press the mixture across the bottom and halfway up the sides of the prepared pan. Refrigerate for at least 15 minutes to firm up the butter. Bake until just set and fragrant, about 10 minutes. Place the pan on a wire rack to cool to room temperature.

3. **For the filling:** Whisk together the condensed milk and egg yolks in a medium bowl. Add the lime juice and whisk until smooth. Pour the filling into the cooled crust. Cover the pan tightly with aluminum foil.

4. Pour 1½ cups water into the pot. Set the dish on a metal trivet with handles and lower them into the pot. Cover and cook on **LOW PRESSURE** for 3 minutes. Let stand for **NATURAL RELEASE** for 5 minutes, then **QUICK RELEASE** the remaining pressure.

5. Remove the dish from the pot, uncover, and let stand on the trivet until cooled to room temperature. Refrigerate until chilled, at least 1 hour. Run a thin knife around the inside the pan to loosen the pie and remove the pan ring before serving.

6. **For the topping:** In a stand mixer fitted with a whisk attachment (or in a large bowl if using a hand mixer), beat the cream, powdered sugar, and vanilla on high speed to firm peaks. Serve the pie with whipped cream and a pinch of flaky salt.

Salted Caramel Banana Pudding

Banana pudding is my favorite Southern dessert that isn't pound cake. Among my pudding principles are an insistence on homemade custard and a strong belief that there is no need for extraneous additions or embellishments. Having said that, I stand behind the addition of a little salted caramel—especially when it is so easy to make the caramel in a multicooker. I like Biscoff cookies in place of traditional 'Nilla wafers, but use the cookie that speaks to you.

Individual servings assembled in drinking glasses or jars are quite cute, and everyone enjoys a dessert that doesn't have to be shared, but you can assemble one large pudding in a 2-quart dish if you prefer. A larger dish might require more cookies.

5 large egg yolks

¼ cup cornstarch

½ cup sugar

¼ teaspoon kosher salt

2 cups whole milk

2 tablespoons unsalted butter, chilled

1 tablespoon vanilla extract

18 Biscoff cookies

¾ cup Salted Caramel (page 160)

2 medium bananas, thinly sliced

HINT *The perfect bananas for this dish are yellow all over with a light freckling of brown spots.*

1. Whisk together the egg yolks, cornstarch, sugar, and salt in a medium bowl until smooth.

2. Warm the milk in the pot on **SAUTÉ LOW** just until it begins to steam; do not let it boil. Whisk about ½ cup of the warm milk into the egg mixture to temper the eggs and then whisk the tempered egg mixture into the pot.

3. Cook the custard while stirring slowly and constantly with a heat-proof spatula until the custard is thick enough to coat the back of the spatula, 3 to 4 minutes. The pot is slightly domed in the center, so make sure you get the spatula into the deeper edges. Turn off the heat. Add the butter and vanilla and stir until smooth.

4. To assemble the puddings, spoon warm custard into six 8-ounce straight-sided glasses or jars to a depth of about ½ inch. Stand 3 Biscoff cookies around the inside of the each glass; the custard will help hold them upright.

5. Spoon 2 tablespoons of Salted Caramel into each glass. Cover with a layer of banana slices. Top with the remaining custard, dividing it evenly among the glasses. Top with more banana slices, if desired. Serve now while still slightly warm, or let cool for 10 minutes, cover each with plastic wrap, and refrigerate until chilled. For the best texture, serve within a day, before the bananas darken.

Salted Caramel

This dulce de leche–style caramel begins with a can of sweetened condensed milk that caramelizes to the color of amber in a water bath inside the multicooker. Some cooks place the can of condensed milk directly in the multicooker, but I prefer to pour it into a wide-mouth jar or glass bowl that fits inside the pot.

This recipe yields twice as much salted caramel needed to make the Salted Caramel Banana Pudding on page 158, but it keeps well for up to a month. You can make up to four batches at once if you need even more caramel, perhaps for gifting (or for yourself, at the end of a hard day). Pour each can of sweetened condensed milk into its own jar and cook them all at the same time. Be sure to arrange the jars on the metal trivet so that their sides don't touch.

1 (14-ounce) can sweetened condensed milk

2 tablespoons unsalted butter

2 tablespoons packed dark brown sugar

1 teaspoon vanilla extract

1 teaspoon kosher salt

1. Pour the condensed milk into a wide-mouth pint jar (or glass bowl) and cover tightly with aluminum foil. Set the jar on a metal trivet with handles and lower them into the pot. Add water to the pot to come halfway up the sides of the jar.

2. Cover and cook on **HIGH PRESSURE** for 45 minutes. Let stand for **NATURAL RELEASE** of the pressure. Remove the jar from the pot and uncover.

3. Add the butter, brown sugar, vanilla, and salt. Whisk vigorously until smooth.

4. Serve warm or let cool to room temperature and then cover tightly and refrigerate for up to 4 weeks.

Strawberry Shortcakes

These casual (but charming) vanilla baby cakes don't form a brown crust as they steam in the multicooker, but they have a firm, tender crumb that reminds me of pound cake or hot milk cake, just right for soaking up strawberry juice without turning soggy. It might be hard to believe you can make homemade cake in ramekins stacked inside a multicooker, but indeed you can.

You can serve the cakes while they are still a little warm, but I think they taste best at room temperature, which means they can be made ahead. After they cool, stash them in an airtight container and keep them on the counter for up to 3 days. (If your kitchen gets hot and humid in the summer, keep the cakes in the fridge and let them return to room temperature before serving.)

For great strawberry shortcake, you also need excellent fresh berries that aren't picked until they are fully ripe and red from tip to cap. The telltale sign of perfect strawberries is their aroma, which perfumes the entire kitchen. You can also make great shortcakes with other ripe, fresh fruits and berries, such as blueberries, raspberries, peaches, and nectarines.

STRAWBERRIES

4 cups hulled and sliced fresh, fragrant, ripe strawberries

6 tablespoons granulated sugar, or to taste

1 tablespoon lemon or orange juice, or to taste

CAKES

Unsalted butter for greasing the ramekins

1 cup all-purpose flour

1 teaspoon baking powder

2 large eggs

1 cup granulated sugar

½ cup whole milk

2 tablespoons unsalted butter

2 teaspoons vanilla extract

TOPPING

1 cup heavy cream, chilled

¼ cup powdered sugar

1 teaspoon vanilla extract, rose water, or orange blossom water

1. **For the strawberries:** Toss together the strawberries and granulated sugar in a bowl. Let stand until needed, stirring occasionally to encourage the berries to release some juice. Just before serving, stir in the lemon juice.

2. **For the cakes:** Butter six 4-ounce ramekins. Whisk together the flour and baking powder in a small bowl.

(recipe continues)

3. In a stand mixer fitted with the paddle attachment (or in a large bowl if using a hand mixer), beat the eggs on high speed until they are thick and pale yellow, about 5 minutes.

4. Add the granulated sugar in a slow, steady stream and continue beating until the mixture doubles in volume and falls in a wide, thick ribbon from the beaters, about 5 minutes.

5. Add the flour mixture and beat on low speed just until smooth. Scrape down the sides of the bowl with a spatula.

6. Warm the milk and butter in a small saucepan over medium heat until the butter melts and the milk begins to steam; do not let the mixture boil. (Alternatively, warm them in a glass measuring cup in the microwave.) Pour into the batter, add the vanilla, and beat on low speed just until smooth.

7. Divide the batter among the prepared ramekins. Cover each ramekin tightly with aluminum foil. Place a metal trivet in the pot and pour in 1½ cups water. Arrange three ramekins on the trivet. Place a second trivet in the pot and arrange the remaining three ramekins on it. Position the top three so that they are not sitting directly above the bottom three. (See the Hint if you do not have a second trivet.) Cover and cook on **HIGH PRESSURE** for 20 minutes. Let stand for **NATURAL RELEASE** for 5 minutes, then **QUICK RELEASE** the remaining pressure.

8. **For the topping:** In a stand mixer fitted with the whisk attachment (or in a large bowl if using a hand mixer), beat the cream, powdered sugar, and vanilla on high speed to firm peaks. Refrigerate until needed.

9. Remove the ramekins from the pot, uncover, run a thin knife around the inside of the ramekins to loosen the cakes, and unmold the cakes onto a wire rack. The cakes can be served warm or at room temperature. To serve, split the cakes horizontally through the middle. Place the bottoms on serving plates, spoon the berries and their juices over them, and replace the tops. Garnish each shortcake with a dollop of whipped cream.

Tres Leches Flan

The steam inside a multicooker replaces the traditional water bath used to make smooth, creamy flan. All you need to do is buzz up the custard base in a blender, pour it into ramekins, and let the pot take over. Although it's possible to cook all six at the same time by stacking them, for even cooking that creates the creamiest flan, cook them three at a time in a single layer. The superior results are worth the additional 9 minutes.

Flan is known for the caramel syrup that flows down their sides when they are turned out of their baking dishes for serving, but if making the caramel seems tedious on a busy day, these are plenty good without it. If you choose to make the caramel, it is easiest to make it in a saucepan on the stovetop. I tried making caramel in the multicooker, but it's not practical to make such a small amount; plus it was difficult to pour the caramel safely into the ramekins.

Flan is not usually served with fruit, but fresh peaches or figs are a delicious accompaniment.

CARAMEL

1¼ cups sugar

FLAN

½ cup cream cheese, at room temperature (4 ounces)

2 large eggs

2 large egg yolks

½ cup sweetened condensed milk

½ cup evaporated milk

½ cup whole milk

1 teaspoon vanilla extract

Pinch of kosher salt

1. **For the caramel:** You must pour the hot caramel into the ramekins before it hardens, so arrange six 4-ounce ramekins on your work surface so that they are ready and waiting. Stir together the sugar and ¼ cup water in a small saucepan. Bring to a simmer over medium-high heat, stirring only until the sugar dissolves. Let cook without stirring until the water evaporates and the sugar syrup thickens and darkens to the color of amber, about 8 minutes. Quickly divide the hot syrup among the ramekins and set aside to cool and harden. (If the caramel hardens before you finish pouring, return the pan to low heat until the caramel liquefies again.)

2. **For the flan:** Combine the cream cheese, eggs, egg yolks, condensed milk, evaporated milk, whole milk, vanilla, and salt in a blender. Blend on low speed until smooth. Let stand until any froth subsides. Strain through a fine-mesh sieve into a large spouted measuring cup (for easy pouring) or a bowl. Divide the custard evenly among the ramekins and cover each tightly with aluminum foil.

3. Pour 1½ cups water into the pot. Set 3 covered ramekins on a metal trivet with handles, spacing them evenly, and lower them into the pot. Cover and cook on **LOW PRESSURE** for 4 minutes. Let stand for **NATURAL RELEASE** for 5 minutes, then **QUICK**

RELEASE the remaining pressure. Transfer the ramekins to a wire cooling rack and remove the foil. The flan will continue to firm up as it cools. Cook the remaining 3 ramekins the same way.

4. Cover the cooled flans and refrigerate until chilled, at least 2 hours and preferably overnight. To serve, run a thin knife blade around the flan to loosen the edges. Working with one at a time, place a serving plate atop a ramekin, and flip them over together. Give a gentle shake so that the flan will drop onto the plate. Lift off the ramekin. Serve chilled.

Lemon Curd

MAKES ABOUT 2 CUPS

Creamy, sweet-tart lemon curd is so versatile (and so easy made in a multicooker)—you can slather it over biscuits, scones, and muffins; spread it between cake layers; swirl it over fresh fruit and cupcakes; spoon it into pie or tart shells; or turn it into Quick Lemon Cream with Fresh Berries (page 166). My favorite lemon curd is made with Meyer lemons that taste like a cross between lemons and mandarin oranges. You can use other citrus too, such as limes, oranges, blood oranges, satsumas, tangerines, or grapefruit.

3 large eggs

4 large egg yolks

1 cup sugar

1 tablespoon finely grated lemon zest

1 cup fresh lemon juice

2 tablespoons unsalted butter, cut into bits and chilled

1. Combine the eggs, egg yolks, sugar, lemon zest, and lemon juice in a blender and process until smooth. Pour into a 1½-quart baking dish and cover tightly with aluminum foil.

2. Pour 1½ cups water into the pot. Set the dish on a metal trivet with handles and lower them into the pot. Cover and cook on **HIGH PRESSURE** for 8 minutes. Let stand for **NATURAL RELEASE** of the pressure.

3. Remove the dish from the pot, uncover, and whisk the curd until smooth. Add the butter and whisk until melted and smooth.

4. Cool, cover, and refrigerate until chilled. Store lemon curd in an airtight container in the refrigerator for up to 2 weeks or frozen for up to 6 months.

Quick Lemon Cream *with Fresh Berries*

MAKES 4 TO 6 SERVINGS

This is my favorite in-a-rush dessert. (I have actually stirred this together in my parked car before carrying it into a party. I'm not kidding.) It requires 3 ingredients, 2 minutes, and 1 bowl. All you have to do is whisk together Lemon Curd (page 165) and Crème Fraîche (page 141), spoon it into serving dishes, toss on some berries, and voilà. Sweet-tart lemon cream tastes remarkably like chilled custard or soft mousse. Sure, you can purchase the lemon curd and crème fraîche, but with a multicooker, those ingredients can easily be homemade, and made ahead. Both lemon curd and crème fraîche keep for weeks in the refrigerator, ready and waiting for when an urgent need (or craving) for a fast dessert strikes.

1 cup lemon curd, preferably homemade Lemon Curd (page 165), chilled

1 cup crème fraîche (homemade, page 141, or store-bought) or sour cream, chilled

4 to 6 cups fresh berries

1. Whisk together the lemon curd and crème fraîche in a medium bowl until well blended and smooth.

2. Spoon into serving bowls, top with berries, and serve chilled. Store in an airtight container in the refrigerator for up to 3 days.

CHOOSING JUICY LEMONS AND LIMES

When choosing lemons, keep in mind that smaller, rounder lemons with thin skins often provide tastier zest and more juice than thick-skinned, football-shaped lemons. When choosing limes for their juice, look for riper limes that have light green or creamy yellow skin, and feel springy when gently squeezed. Save those hard, bright-green limes for when you need zest for looks instead of flavor. A good trick for getting the most juice from lemons and limes, no matter their ripeness or size, is to microwave them for 20 seconds to soften them a bit.

166 - *Instantly* Southern

Fresh Apple and Black Walnut Cake
with Brown Sugar Glaze

This type of fresh apple cake hails from my beloved Blue Ridge Mountains where heirloom apples and black walnuts reign during autumn and are often used together in desserts. Not everyone is fond of the distinct tannic, earthy flavor of black walnuts, however, so you can use English walnuts if you prefer. The cake is moist (even more so when steamed in a multicooker) and bathed in a warm brown sugar glaze that sets up like soft penuche candy as it cools. It's simply fantastic, and reminds us that a cake doesn't have to be made in layers and coated in buttercream to be stunning.

CAKE

Unsalted butter and all-purpose flour for the pan

1½ cups all-purpose flour

2 teaspoons apple pie spice

¾ teaspoon baking powder

½ teaspoon baking soda

¼ teaspoon kosher salt

8 tablespoons unsalted butter, melted

½ cup granulated sugar

½ cup packed light brown sugar

2 large eggs

1 large egg yolk

½ cup sour cream

1 teaspoon vanilla extract

2 cups peeled and diced apples (about ½-inch pieces)

½ cup black walnut pieces

1. **For the cake:** Butter and flour a 7-inch round pan. Whisk together the flour, apple pie spice, baking powder, baking soda, and salt in a medium bowl until well blended.

2. In a stand mixer fitted with the paddle attachment (or in a large bowl if using a hand mixer), beat the melted butter, granulated sugar, and brown sugar on high speed until light and creamy, about 5 minutes.

3. Add the eggs and egg yolk, one at a time, beating well and scraping down the bowl after each addition. Beat in the sour cream and vanilla.

4. Add half of the flour mixture and beat on low speed only until smooth. Scrape the sides of the bowl with a spatula. Add the remaining flour mixture and beat just until smooth. Scrape the bowl to make sure all of the flour mixture is incorporated. Fold in the apples and walnuts, and then transfer the cake batter to the prepared pan. Cover the pan tightly with aluminum foil.

(recipe continues)

GLACE AND TOPPING

2 tablespoons
unsalted butter

2 tablespoons packed
light brown sugar

2 tablespoons
granulated sugar

¼ teaspoon salt

¼ cup heavy cream

½ teaspoon vanilla extract

½ cup black walnut pieces

5. Pour 1½ cups water into the pot. Set the pan on a metal trivet with handles and lower them into the pot. Cover and cook on **HIGH PRESSURE** for 60 minutes. Let stand for **NATURAL RELEASE** for 10 minutes, then **QUICK RELEASE** any remaining pressure. Remove the cake from the pot, uncover, and let cool in the pan on the trivet for 20 minutes.

6. **For the glaze:** Melt the butter in a small saucepan over medium heat. Add the brown sugar, granulated sugar, and salt. Stir until smooth and simmer for 2 minutes.

7. Stir in the cream, bring to a boil, and cook until the glaze thickens, about 5 minutes, stirring slowly and constantly. Remove the pan from the heat and stir in the vanilla. Let stand until the cake cools. The glaze will continue to thicken a bit as it cools.

8. Run a thin knife around the inside of the pan to loosen the cake and turn it out onto a serving plate. Turn the cake top-side up. Poke holes at 1-inch intervals over the top of the cake with a wooden skewer or chopstick. Slowly pour the glaze over the cake, letting some of it seep down into the holes. Arrange the walnuts over the top. Let stand until the glaze sets before serving.

Blackberry Bread Pudding
with Easy Grand Marnier Sauce

It's hard to beat fresh blackberries in the summer, although frozen berries make this dish an option year-round. It's a flexible recipe, so you can use other berries, such as strawberries, raspberries, or a medley. You can also replace the rich, eggy challah bread with cubes of store-bought frozen pound cake.

The creamy Grand Marnier sauce sounds fancy, but is nothing more than melted premium vanilla ice cream with an added splash of orange liqueur and orange zest.

PUDDING

Unsalted butter for
the baking dish

2 large eggs

2 large egg yolks

2 cups half-and-half

½ cup sugar

1 tablespoon Grand Marnier

2 teaspoons finely
grated orange zest

2 teaspoons vanilla extract

5 cups lightly packed cubed
or torn challah (6 ounces)

1 cup fresh or thawed
blackberries

GRAND MARNIER SAUCE

1 pint premium vanilla ice cream

½ cup Grand Marnier,
or to taste

2 teaspoons finely
grated orange zest

Fresh blackberries,
for garnish (optional)

1. **For the pudding:** Butter a 1½-quart round baking dish. Whisk the eggs and egg yolks in a large bowl until well blended. Whisk in the half-and-half, sugar, Grand Marnier, orange zest, and vanilla. Stir in the bread and let stand at room temperature for 10 minutes, stirring occasionally to help the bread fully absorb the custard.

2. Pour half of the bread mixture into the dish. Add all the berries in an even layer, then the rest of the bread mixture. Cover the dish tightly with aluminum foil. Refrigerate for at least 1 hour and up to overnight.

3. Pour 1½ cups water into the pot. Set the baking dish on a metal trivet with handles and lower them into the pot. Cover and cook on **HIGH PRESSURE** for 25 minutes. Let stand for **NATURAL RELEASE** for 20 minutes, then **QUICK RELEASE** the remaining pressure.

4. While the pudding cooks, let the ice cream sit at room temperature to melt.

5. **For the sauce:** In a medium bowl, whisk together the melted ice cream, Grand Marnier, and zest until combined.

6. Remove the pudding from the pot, uncover, and let stand for at least 20 minutes before serving warm or at room temperature with the sauce and a few fresh berries, if using. Lightly chilled leftovers aren't too bad either, and tend to be more pleasing than reheated leftovers that can turn gummy.

Acknowledgments

It takes a village (several, actually) to create a book. I'm deeply grateful for the talents and support of everyone involved, and would like to mention a few in particular.

Raquel Pelzel, my editor, who launched this project and brought it in for a safe landing.

Sarah Smith of the David Black Agency, my literary agent and friend, who always keeps the big picture in view, including my spot in it.

The team who tested, tasted, schlepped, swept, proofed, and propped me up through the process: Cathy Barrow, Kim Calaway, Lisa Carl, Susan Dosier, Anne Dusek, Keebe Fitch, Jonette Futch, Kendra Haden, Catherine Linford, Keia Mastriani, Mary Brooks Seagroves, Athina Sgambati, Judy Shertzer—and most of all, the incomparable Marah Stets.

The photography and style team: Hélène Dujardin, Kim Phillips, Tami Hardeman, and Abby Gaskins.

The design, production, marketing, PR, and sales teams at Clarkson Potter and Penguin Random House who weld their considerable talents to transform a manuscript into an actual book and get it into the hands of readers. Let me give particular thanks to Catherine Casalino, Marysarah Quinn, Stephanie Huntwork, Mark McCauslin, Kim Tyner, Heather Williamson, Kate Tyler, Natasha Martin, and Elora Sullivan.

Beloved companions: Thimble, Pepita, and Wren.

The musicians who serve as my sound track while I work on a book, especially Jason Isbell and John Prine this time around. You have an everlasting dinner invitation.

To home cooks and cookbook readers everywhere. We're all in this together.

Index

About the Author

SHERI CASTLE is a Chapel Hill–based cookbook author, recipe developer, and cooking teacher. She coauthored both the *Southern Living Community Cookbook* and the *Southern Foodways Alliance Community Cookbook;* her cookbook, *The New Southern Garden Cookbook,* was named Cookbook of the Year by the Southern Independent Booksellers' Association. Sheri is a frequent contributor to *Southern Living, The Kitchn,* and many others.

"Sheri has always had the unique ability to anticipate just what it is we're craving. She's arrived right on time to satisfy our hunger for fresh Southern food with the help of the multicooker. I'm going to cook my way through this book, and the Hoppin' John Risotto is where I plan to start!"

HALI BEY RAMDENE
food director, *The Kitchn*

"I trust Sheri Castle's Southern kitchen know-how so much that I would gladly spend a whole weekend on a recipe she crafted. It's just gravy that she's applied that same expertise to multicooker recipes so it only takes a fraction of the time to get them to the table. And even better—there are plenty of recipes for actual gravy!"

KAT KINSMAN
senior food and drinks editor, ExtraCrispy.com